RUBBER band GLAM

A Rainbow of Dazzling Beaded Designs for Bracelets, Accessories, and More

Christina Friedrichsen-Truman,
Emily Truman, and
Madeline Truman

Quarry Books
100 Cummings Center, Suite 406L
Beverly, MA 01915

quarrybooks.com • www.craftside.net

First published in the United States of America in 2015 by

Quarry Books, a member of

Quarto Publishing Group USA Inc.

100 Cummings Center

Suite 406-L

Beverly, Massachusetts 01915-6101

Telephone: (978) 282-9590

Fax: (978) 283-2742

www.quarrybooks.com

Visit www.craftside.net for a behind-the-scenes peek at our crafty world!

10 9 8 7 6 5 4 3 2 1

ISBN: 978-1-63159-060-3

Digital edition published in 2015

eISBN: 978-1-62788-345-0

Library of Congress Cataloging-in-Publication Data is available

Design: Mattie Wellls

Beauty Shot Photographer: Christina Friedrichsen-Truman

Instructions Writer/Steps Photographer: Michelle Barnes

Illustrator: Uli Monch

Printed in China

Christina:
For my daughters, Emily and Madeline,
who never cease to amaze me.

Emily and Madeline:
For our dad, who can fix anything.

Contents

Preface

LOOM CRAZY!

You never know when something will show up in your life, setting you off on a brand new adventure. It might, for instance, show up in your mailbox on a dull, chilly afternoon wrapped in plain kraft paper, bearing the familiar handwriting of a loved one. Even after you tear it open, it may fail to pique your interest any more than watching golf on television.

It was September 2013 when a Rainbow Loom made its not-so-grand entrance into our home. It was a birthday gift for my youngest daughter, Madeline (then eight years old), from her aunt Tracy in Toronto. I had never heard of Rainbow Loom. I took one look at the plastic device, and I wrote it off as something that would end up in the back of her closet. Or the Rainbow Loom might even get tossed into the donation box. My oldest daughter, Emily, who was ten at the time, had received a friendship bracelet maker the year before. After several failed attempts at creating the beautiful woven bracelets shown on the outside of the box, the contraption was shipped off to our nearest Goodwill. Rainbow Loom wouldn't be too far behind, or so I thought.

Fast forward one month, and we barely had room to eat at our kitchen table. Rainbow Loom had cast a spell over us, and there was no turning back. Towering stacks of storage cases filled with rubber bands in every color had nearly taken over our entire eating space. And then there were the bracelets themselves, which threatened to overtake the one small, tidy area of the kitchen table that we had reserved for meal time. TV trays, here we come!

Nearly every day after school, Emily and Madeline would make a beeline for the kitchen table, where they would loom their hearts out until suppertime. Minecraft, which up until that time was more addictive to them than potato chips, was a distant memory. In fact, iPods now served only one purpose: to advance looming skills. Countless videos on YouTube gave the girls the opportunity to do just that.

The thing that blew me away about all of this was how quickly the girls were able to crack the code on rubber band bracelet making. Before long, they were inventing their own bracelet patterns. In fact, it wasn't long before their original designs were flying off the loom daily—sometimes hourly. That's when I had my eureka moment.

I knew there were countless YouTube channels devoted to rubber band looming, but there wasn't a website devoted to loom tutorials, other than the official Rainbow Loom company site. On October 1, 2013, LoomLove.com was born.

Since that fateful day, LoomLove.com has had more than six million visitors from around the world. Many of our visitors have turned into devoted fans, frequenting the site daily for new tutorials. In an effort to keep these loyal loomers happy, we wanted to find something new to create with our looms. When our publisher approached us with the idea of creating a book about beaded rubber band jewelry designs, we decided to give it a whirl, using exclusively glass beads. The results were amazing! The more we experimented, the more we were convinced that we had to share this eye candy (or wrist candy!) with our fans in book form.

Rubber Band Glam is perfect for avid loomers who are looking for a new way to use their looms, and it's also ideal for anyone who is new to the craft. Several of the designs in this book are easy, perfect for anyone just starting out, while more advanced loomers will find more challenging designs to keep them engaged in this fun craft.

Even if you've put your loom away, *Rubber Band Glam* will inspire you to dig it out of storage and get excited about looming again. After all, you'll be creating designs that are unlike anything you've ever made out of rubber bands.

We used glass beads for all the projects in this book. We've seen rubber band bracelets with plastic beads, but we don't think they have the same "wow" factor as glass beads. That said, if you only have access to plastic beads, you can still complete all the projects in this book.

Happy looming, everyone!

Ten Reasons Why We Love Rubber Band Looming

Rubber band looming with beads is fabulous for so many reasons.
Here are our top ten reasons why we think it's awesome.

I. It inspires creativity. Coming up with color combinations and patterns is a fun, creative process. There's an endless variety of color combinations and bracelet patterns to discover, and adding beads brings a whole new dimension to rubber band bracelet making.

2. It inspires learning. Rubber band looming teaches kids how to follow step-by-step instructions, and it rewards loomers for paying close attention to the details with a cool project to show off.

3. It inspires sharing. Kids share their fabulous creations, and they also share information with each other about how to create various bracelet patterns. Anything that motivates kids to help each other gets a big ol' thumbs up from us!

4. It's challenging. One of the best things about rubber band looming is that once you've mastered one pattern, there's always a new and more challenging pattern to tackle. Adding beads to patterns kicks it up a notch.

5. It builds confidence. We find it exhilarating when we've created a new beaded loom project that we love. This builds confidence to keep going with more challenging designs.

6. It rewards perseverance. It's amazing how fiercely determined we can be when we are trying to master new patterns. When a pattern doesn't work out the first time, we keep going, knowing the reward of a new beaded rubber band creation is waiting for us at the end.

7. It's a quiet activity. When we're creating bracelets, we're completely immersed in our activity. We're so immersed, in fact, that we usually don't make a peep—except for the odd outburst when something goes wrong.

8. It offers a new and exciting way to use technology. Instead of using electronic devices to play video games, children use technology to watch instructional videos on how to create loom bracelets. We believe this is the perfect marriage of old and new. Combining technology with hands-on activities is the way of the future.

9. It's inexpensive. Compared to smart phones, tablets, and other techno gadgets, rubber band looming isn't hard on the pocketbook.

10. The beaded creations are beautiful. What girl doesn't love a little sparkle in her life?

Rubber
BAND
LOOMING
Essentials

The Basics

When we created our first rubber band loom bracelet with glass beads, we did a little happy dance. The bracelet was pure eye candy, and it was also easy to make. Perhaps best of all, it didn't require special jewelry-making tools, such as crimpers, pliers, or wire cutters.

That's truly the beauty of *Rubber Band Glam*. All of the gorgeous designs in this book (aside from the earrings, which require either split rings or jump rings and earring wire) can be made by both kids and adults. And no looming experience is necessary.

The variety of beads that can be used is truly endless. You can even thread tiny glass seed beads onto the bands. Beads that are round, square, oval, and diamond-shaped are all suitable. In fact, as long as the hole of the bead is big enough to thread a rubber band through, you're good to go.

You can use a variety of beads, and many of the existing loom bracelet patterns work

exceptionally well with beads. If you want to change up the look of some of your favorite bracelet designs, simply add beads. Most of the designs in this book are Loom Love original designs. After lots of experimenting, we chose the ones that looked the best.

THE LEARNING CURVE

If you're new to rubber band looming, you'll find there's a bit of a learning curve. Some designs, such as the Beaded Single Bracelet (see page 30) or the Beaded Fishtail Bracelet (see page 38), are easy to nail on your first try, while others, like the Whirlwind Bracelet (page 103), may take a few attempts.

Once you have a handful of bracelets under your belt, you'll start to understand the method behind placing your bands and the fundamentals of hooking the bands properly. If you're a crocheter, you'll have a head start. In fact, several rubber band looming superstars have backgrounds in crochet.

LOOMS

We use a Rainbow Loom. In fact, we use two of them for several projects in this book. But there are several other looms on the market that you can use for many of our projects, including Cra-Z-Loom, FunLoom, and Wonder Loom. With that said, Cra-Z-Loom, FunLoom, and Wonder Loom don't have removable rows, which means it won't be possible to make some of the designs in this book on those looms, such as the Cute Coin Purse (see page 132).

While you can make the projects in this book using only one loom, we recommend a second loom. Many of the single-loom bracelets require that you add an extension so it fits around your wrist, while two-loom bracelets look more finished and fit all the way around your wrist. (If you will be using a single loom, we teach you how to make extensions on page 19.)

The majority of the projects in this book are made on a Rainbow Loom; however, the Chandelier Bracelet (see page 120), Chandelier Earrings (see page 125), and Bead Garden Bracelet (see page 129) are created using a hook.

The first photo (A) shows the Jane Austen bracelet (see page 48) with an extension. It was made using a single loom. The second photo (B) shows the same bracelet design made on two looms, without an extension.

Loom Love's Looms

How many looms does Loom Love own? The answer: Five! That way, Maddie, Emily, and Christina (mom) can all loom together, although Christina admits she is much better at photographing the designs than she is at making them.

HOOKS

A plastic hook comes with most rubber band looms. Because they are plastic, they snap easily. In fact, we broke five plastic hooks prior to purchasing our official Rainbow Loom metal upgrade hook. We prefer the Rainbow Loom metal hook to any of the other hooks we've used, including metal crochet hooks. The groove in the official Rainbow Loom hook is deeper than the groove in the crochet hooks we've tried, and consequently, the bands don't slip off the hook as easily.

If you decide to purchase a crochet hook for looming, a size G-6/4.25 mm is best for the projects in this book.

CLIPS

To close your designs, you will need either plastic C-clips or S-clips. Official Rainbow Loom bands come with C-clips, while most other brands come with S-clips. Both types of closures work well for all of the bracelet designs in this book.

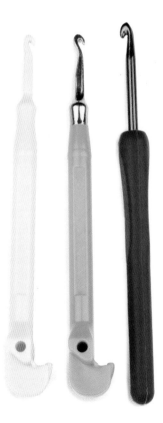

Here are a variety of hooks that can be used for rubber band looming.

Both C-clips [A] and S-clips [B] can be used as closures for the bracelet designs in this book.

Let's Get Looming

This section includes everything you need to know about working with a rubber band loom.

LOOM CONFIGURATIONS

There are two basic loom configurations that we use for our projects: the *offset or staggered* configuration and the *rectangular or even* configuration.

If you're using a Cra-Z-Loom, Fun Loom, or Wonder Loom, the pegs are fixed and set in the staggered configuration.

Offset or staggered configuration. All Rainbow Looms are sold in the offset configuration. When the loom is positioned so the red arrow is facing away from you, the middle peg bar is offset a half peg back from the rows on either side of it.

Rectangular or even configuration. In this configuration, all the rows of pegs line up.

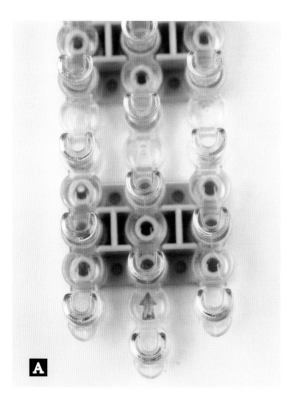

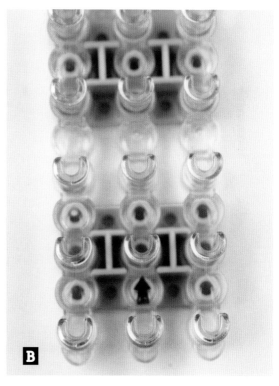

The Rainbow Loom is shown here in the staggered or offset configuration (A) and the rectangular or even configuration (B).

USING MORE THAN ONE LOOM

We used two looms attached end to end to make several bracelet projects in this book so they're long enough to fit around your wrist. If you don't have two looms, see "How to add an extension to a bracelet" on page 19 for details on how to create and attach an extension for a bracelet design.

To attach two looms together in an end-to-end configuration, you'll need the base removal tool, which can be found on the end of your Rainbow Loom hook. (If you're making something really long, like a necklace or a belt, you can also use this technique to attach more than two looms.)

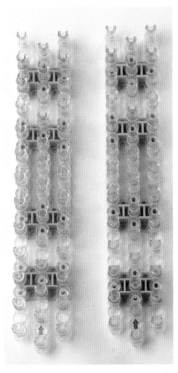

I. Position both looms so the red arrows are facing away from you.

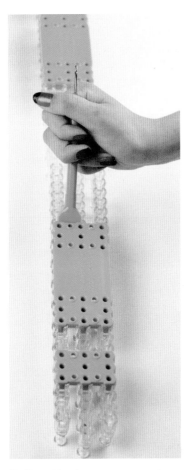

2. Turn the looms over and place them end to end. Using your base removal tool, remove one small base from one loom and one small base and a large base from the second loom.

3. Center the large base where the two looms meet and press it firmly into place.

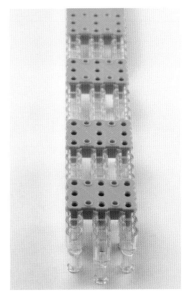

4. Place the two small bases onto the bottom loom, three rows apart.

LOOMING FUNDAMENTALS

This section offers an overview of how to make the most important elements of a rubber band loom project.

How to make a cap band. One of the most important components of a loom bracelet is the cap band, which is a band that is double-looped. Without a cap band, your project will fall apart. Most projects have one cap band, while other designs require more than one. Often the cap band is the last band you'll place on your loom before looping the bands.

I. Place your band on the peg.

2. Make a figure eight shape with your band.

3. Loop the figure eight over your peg.

A Key to the Looming Illustrations

Each loom project includes illustrations that show how bands and beads are placed and looped. Here's what the colors and shapes used in the illustrations mean.

Green arrows and bands: These show the direction and sequence of placing the bands and beads.

Yellow and orange circles: These indicate the placement of a bead; they do not reflect the actual color of the bead(s) used.

Black arrows: These show the direction and sequence of looping the bands.

Blue arrows and bands: Used only in few projects, these indicate a secondary set of moves, which are specified in the accompanying instructions. They may appear in either the placing or looping illustrations.

Zigzag or jagged lines across a loom: These are used to indicate that a part of the loom is not shown but the pattern for either placing or looping bands should be continued according to the instructions.

How to make a slip knot. Several of our projects require adding a slip knot after the bands have been hooked or looped in order to hold the open bands in place before taking the project off the loom. To do this, you'll need a band and a hook.

I. Place both ends of the band over your hook.

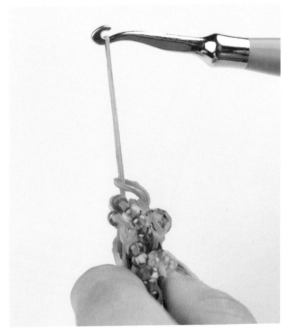

3. Pull the slip knot band taut to gather the open bands together.

2. Place the hook through the open band or bands and then place the right side of the slip knot band over the left side.

How to add an extension to a bracelet. Several projects in this book are made on two looms so they're long enough to fit around your wrist, while others use an extension. If you don't have two looms, you'll need to make an extension for several of the bracelet designs in this book; otherwise, they won't fit around your wrist.

I. Remove your project from the loom, leaving the open band(s) on the hook.

3. Carefully remove your bracelet from the hook and place it on the last peg that's holding an extension band.

5. Grab the last extension band with your hook while pushing back the bands above it (the bands that are attached to your bracelet) with the back of your hook. Pull the band up and over the next peg. Repeat until you reach the end of the loom.

2. Position the loom so the red arrow is pointing away from you and then place several bands on the loom along one row of pegs. Six bands work best for most bracelets, depending on the size of your wrist.

4. Reposition the loom so the red arrow is pointing toward you. Place your hook into the channel of the first peg. When looping your bands, always make sure the open side of the hook is facing away from you.

6. Add a C-clip or an S-clip to the last loop.

7. Pull your finished project off of the loom and attach the clip to the cap band on the other end of the bracelet.

Strike Up the Band

For us, the loom band section of a store is almost as fun as scouring the goodies aisle for our favorite candy. We love it when we discover a new loom band color or style. Loom bands are to loomers what a palette is to a painter: the wider the palette, the more opportunity there is for exploration and creativity.

Most loom bands are made of either synthetic latex-free rubber or silicone and are sold in packages of 300 or 600. Although most of the loom bands in our collection are official Rainbow Loom brand synthetic rubber bands, we also have many other types of loom bands. For the most part, we find that official Rainbow Loom bands last longer and don't break as easily (and they're guaranteed to be latex-free); however, many of the other loom bands in our collection work perfectly for bracelets. Shown here are some of the different varieties of loom bands.

Solid. These are classic and a staple in many loomers' collections. They're opaque and come in a wide variety of colors.

Silicone. These are made of silicone instead of synthetic rubber so they don't break down as quickly. They're also stain-resistant and, according to official Rainbow Loom, "impervious to almost any liquid or environmental condition." We've found they don't stretch as well as synthetic rubber bands, which can make them more difficult to work with, especially when they're used in more challenging designs.

Clear. We discovered these a few months into our loom obsession and now we can't live without them. Many of our favorite designs look their finest with the addition of clear bands, and they also look phenomenal in beaded projects. We strongly suggest that you get your hands on some! (Ours are official Rainbow Loom brand.)

Jelly. Sold in a wide assortment of colors, jelly bands (which are transparent, like jelly) are used in several projects in this book.

Tie-dye. Tie-dye bands are more than one color—usually two, one main color with large, random flecks of another—and are sold in a variety of color combinations. They can add a fun effect to many rubber band loom designs.

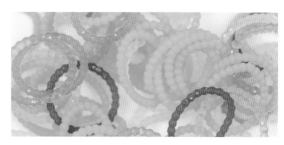

Bubble. The bumpy edges on these bands create a neat effect in many designs. Every time we post a bracelet using bubble bands (also called beaded bands) on LoomLove.com, we get a deluge of inquiries about them.

Polka dot. Like tie-dye bands, polka dot bands are usually two colors, but the colors alternate in a regular pattern—they're also sometimes called poker chip bands for that reason.

Glow-in-the-dark. Glow-in-the-dark bands are available in white as well as in other colors. Turn the lights off, and you'll see how they'll make your projects glow. They're a fun addition to a collection, but they're not used in any of the projects.

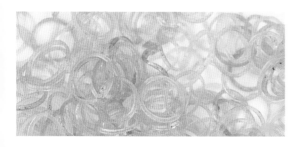

Glitter. To add even more sparkle to your loom projects, you can use glitter bands along with beads. (We used them in our Spring Bouquet Bracelet; see page 57.)

Color-changing. When exposed to ultraviolet light, these bands change color. They're not used for any of the projects in this book, but you can buy them online.

Metallic. Metallic bands are some of our favorites, and we highly recommend them for beaded loom projects. You can buy several varieties of metallic bands, including silver, gold, bronze, and colored metallic bands. Check out our Beaded Lantern Bracelet (see page 95) to see them in action.

Pastel. Pastels didn't show up on the scene until we were almost a year into looming. They quickly became some of our favorites. They're currently sold in mixed packages.

Pearl. Pearl bands, which are made of silicone, have a pearl-like sheen. They're available in a variety of colors from the official Rainbow Loom USA webstore.

Persian. Similar to pastels, Persian bands didn't show up until we were many months into our looming adventure. Because of their gold, metallic sheen, Persian bands are perfect for adding bling to your designs, and they are ideal for beaded projects.

Neon. We love our neon loom bands! Neon bands come in hot pink, lime green, yellow, orange, purple, and blue. They add a wonderful pop of color to your bracelets—whether or not you're using beads.

ORGANIZING YOUR BANDS

Plastic storage containers are the best containers in which to organize your loom bands. Unless you want to spend a bundle on your containers, stay away from plastic storage units that are sold specifically as rubber band organizers. Instead, head to your local hardware store.

We purchased our first few cases in the hardware section of our local dollar store, but we outgrew them pretty quickly. During a trip to a hardware store, we discovered a plastic organizer made by Stanley. The instant we set eyes on it, we knew that it was a match made in heaven for our loom band collection. The sections are dividable and deep with lots of room for bands. Another bonus is that you can stack the cases on top of one another and lock them in place. We highly recommend this case for avid loomers.

Using a repurposed tool organizer is a great way to sort and store your loom bands.

SORTING YOUR BANDS

When it comes to sorting our bands, we prefer to organize them by color. We have a large collection of bands, and things can get out of hand pretty fast, so we try to make sure we always put our bands in their proper places when we're done working with them.

Also, always make sure your loom band cases are completely closed when you put them away. We made the mistake once of not completely closing one of our cases, and we ended up with a big mess of bands on the kitchen floor.

Speaking of rubber bands on the floor: Make sure you don't leave any stray bands lying around. They can be a hazard to your pets as well as to small children who might put them in their mouths.

The Loom Love Band Collection

We have so many different types and colors of bands that we sort and store them by both color and by type.

Emily's Top Five Fave Band Colors

1. Solid teal
2. Solid olive green
3. Neon pink
4. Persian bands (any color)
5. Clear

Madeline's Top Five Fave Band Colors

1. Solid pink
2. Bubble band blue
3. Metallic gold
4. Jelly pink
5. Clear

Just Bead It

When we began experimenting with adding beads to our rubber band bracelets, we quickly realized how dramatically they can change the look of a loom bracelet. A bracelet design will look radically different after adding beads, and the type of beads will completely alter the look. For instance, beads in geometric shapes (such as the Triple Single Bracelet, page 34) will look very different from patterned beads (Dot to Dot Bracelet, page 37). Playing around with bead combinations is one of the best things about creating beaded loom designs.

Although beads can be made of plastic, clay, acrylic, wood, and even stone, we used primarily glass beads for the projects in this book. We didn't use plastic beads in any of the designs in this book. As we mentioned earlier, you can substitute them if you don't have access to fancier beads. You can use plastic pony beads, Perler Beads, and other types of plastic beads in these designs, but obviously they'll give the designs a much different look.

Most of the beads used for the projects in this book are Halcraft Bead Gallery beads, which you can find at major craft retailers. We also used Darice Japanese seed beads, which you can purchase both online and at craft retailers.

We also found our local dollar store to be a treasure trove for inexpensive glass beaded bracelets. After purchasing the bracelets, we simply dismantled the bracelets, removing each of the beads for use in our projects. You might even have some beaded jewelry around your home that you no longer use. Why not recycle it for your beaded loom band projects?

Because of the endless variety of shapes, colors, and sizes of beads that are available, the possibilities are endless when it comes to beaded rubber band designs. Here are a few of the bead types that we think work particularly well with beaded loom band projects.

Faceted glass. These beads are cut and polished, making them sparkle when they catch the light. They are perfect for adding elegance to your loom creations. We used faceted glass beads in an array of colors, oftentimes pairing them with other bead styles in matching colors.

Glass seed. We let out a little shriek of delight the first time we slid a rubber band through a glass seed bead. We honestly didn't think a band would fit through the hole. We love how seed beads look on rubber band designs. We used 6/0 "E" Premium Darice Japanese seed beads for the projects in this book.

Millefiori glass. There are a myriad of patterns when it comes to beads. Among our favorites are from Bead Gallery's millefiori collection (shown far left and center). Pairing these beads with clear bands allows the beads' gorgeous patterns to take center stage in your designs.

Geometric shapes. When it comes to beads, round is definitely not your only option. Squares, ovals, triangles, and cylinders are just a few of the geometric shapes available to you.

Metallic colors. Beads in gold, silver, and copper colors look amazing on loom bracelet designs, especially when paired with metallic bands. Beads in metallic colors come in a vast array of shapes and sizes, and they are perfect for creating a variety of bracelet styles, from tribal to modern.

Crystal. These gorgeous beads, which come in a wide variety of shapes and sizes, look especially lovely when paired with white or clear rubber bands.

STORING YOUR BEADS

You can store your beads in many ways. You can use clear bags, small glass or plastic containers, or storage cases. Aside from our glass seed beads, which we leave in their original containers, we store our beads in plastic storage cases that we purchased from our local craft store.

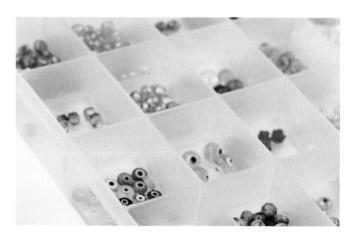

HOW TO ADD BEADS TO YOUR BRACELETS

Adding beads to rubber bands is easy-peasy. All you need is some fishing line, nylon, or even dental floss. If your beads were strung when you purchased them, you can even use the string that they came on. You can add one or more beads to a rubber band using the following method.

I. Insert the nylon thread through the bead hole.

3. Fold the thread over the band and then pass the end of the thread back through the bead hole.

2. Place a band on the end of the thread.

4. Use the doubled thread to gently pull the band through the bead hole until the bead sits in the middle of the band.

Banding Your Beads

We bead all of our bands ahead of time. It seems to go quicker that way—especially for more complicated projects that require lots of beads, such as the Bead Garden Bracelet (see page 129).

Finishing Touches

You'll be sure to get lots of compliments on your *Rubber Band Glam* collection of bracelets. When you're not showing them off by wearing them, there are numerous ways that you can display your creations.

Keep in mind that rubber bands will break down over time when they're exposed to the air. We suggest that when you're not displaying your bracelets, you store them in airtight containers or sealed plastic bags.

You can buy bracelet displays online and from your local craft store. They come in a variety of styles and colors. We use a white velveteen bracelet display for our beaded rubber band bracelets.

LoomLove.com Video Tutorial

At the end of each project, you'll see a QR code like the one here. To see an online video demonstration of that project, scan the QR code using a QR code reader app on a smart phone or tablet, or upload a photo of it to an online QR code reader. You can also access the videos by typing either loomlove.com or quarrybooks.com/pages/rubberbandglam into your browser, then the name of the project as noted on page 142.

Rubber BAND GLAM DESIGNS

Beaded Single Bracelet

If you're new to beaded loom projects, the Beaded Single Bracelet is the place to start. This bracelet is super easy. For this design, we used large glass millefiori-style beads along with delicate Japanese glass seed beads. Clear bands make the colors pop.

Level of Difficulty

» Easy (Great for Beginners)

What You'll Need

» 60 clear bands
» 15 to 20 6 mm glass beads in various colors (Halcraft's Bead Gallery Glass millefiori)
» 15 to 20 round Japanese glass seed beads in blue
» 1 C-clip or S-clip
» 1 loom
» 1 hook

Loom Configuration

This bracelet is made using any two pegs on an outside row of the loom.

Banding the Beads

Following the instructions on page 26, place all the beads on the clear bands. The number of beaded bands you'll need to complete the bracelet will depend on the circumference of your wrist.

MAKING THE BRACELET

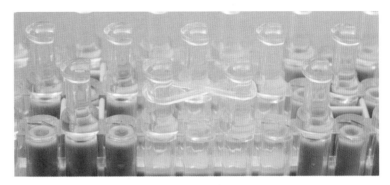

I. Place a single clear band in a figure eight pattern on two pegs anywhere along an outside row of the loom.

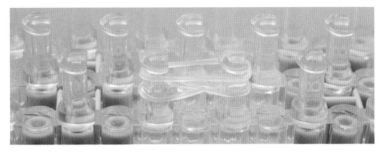

2. Place a second single band over the figure eight.

3. Hook the figure eight band from the outer right side and bring it over the peg to the center.

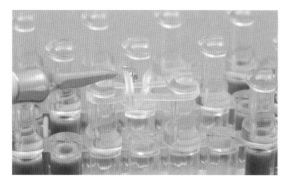

4. Repeat step 3 on the left side.

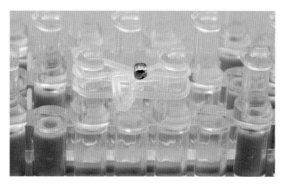

5. Place a banded seed bead over the previous bands.

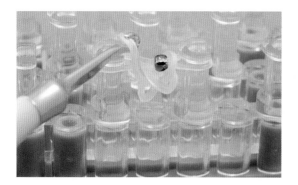

6. Hook the bottom band on the right side and bring it over the peg to the center. Repeat on the left side.

7. Place a large banded bead on the pegs. Hook the bottom band over the pegs as before. Alternating seed beads and long beads, continue the pattern until the bracelet is long enough to fit around your wrist.

8. Place a single clear band over the pegs. Hook the bottom band over the top band.

9. Hook the remaining band off the right peg and loop it over the left peg.

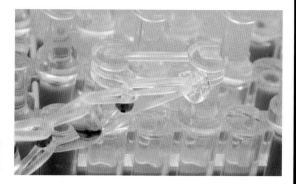

10. Stretch the last band back onto the right peg. Add a C-clip or S-clip and remove the bracelet from the loom.

Variation

Green Glitter Bracelet

You can dramatically change the look of the Beaded Single design by using different bands and beads. To create the Green Glitter design, we used pastel and olive green bands and a gorgeous green faceted Bead Gallery bead. Use the supplies listed below and follow the instructions on the preceding pages.

Beads and Bands

» 30 pastel bands in various colors

» 30 solid olive green bands

» 45 to 60 faceted glass beads in green (Halcraft's Bead Gallery Painted Glass Rondelles)

LoomLove.com
Video Tutorial

Beaded Triple Single Bracelet

The Triple Single is a classic bracelet design in the looming world. We think it looks amazing with beads. We paired large, flat round beads with smaller square beads. The combination of the two shapes gives the bracelet a fun, modern, geometric look.

Level of Difficulty
» Easy

What You'll Need
» 75 solid teal bands

» 15 clear bands

» 12 flat round glass beads in iridescent teal (Halcraft's Bead Gallery Glass millefiori)

» 24 square glass beads in iridescent teal

» 3 C-clips or S-clips

» 1 loom

» 1 hook

Loom Configuration
Rectangular/even

Banding the Beads
Following the instructions on page 26, place all of the beads on the teal bands.

PLACING THE BANDS AND BEADS

1. Position the loom so the red arrow is pointing away from you. Place a square beaded band on pegs 1 and 4. Continue placing square beaded bands on the same vertical row, from pegs 4 to 7, 7 to 10, and so on, until you reach the top of the loom.

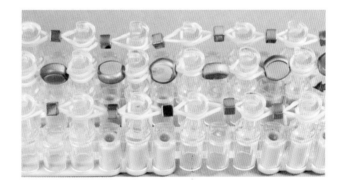

2. Place the round beaded bands along the center row in the same pattern, the first from pegs 2 to 5, then from pegs 5 to 8, continuing to the end of the loom. Using the remaining square beaded bands, repeat this same pattern on the last row. Steps 1 and 2 are shown in illustration A.

A

LOOPING THE BANDS

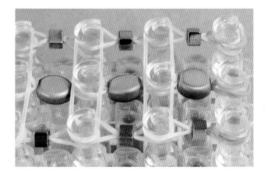

3. Place the clear bands around the horizontal rows of pegs, starting with pegs 4, 5, and 6. Repeat on all horizontal rows, ending on pegs 34, 35, and 36. This step is shown in illustration B.

4. Reposition the loom so the red arrow is pointing toward you. Place a cap band on pegs 37, 38, and 39.

5. Hook the beaded band from under the cap band on peg 39 and loop it forward to peg 36. Repeat this pattern along that vertical row, from peg 36 to 33, from 33 to 30, and so on, until you reach the other end of the loom. Steps 4 and 5 are shown in illustration C.

B

C

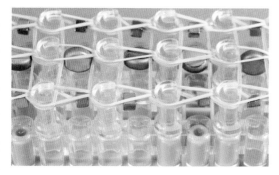

6. Repeat this pattern on the center and right-hand vertical rows.

7. Hook through both bands on peg I and then take another band and hook it through, using a toothpick to hold the added band. Repeat this step on pegs 2 and 3. Then, holding the three toothpicks and loops, remove your bracelet from the loom. Following the instructions on page 19, create an extension for your bracelet so it fits around your wrist. We created a triple extension to correspond to the three rows of this design. Add a C-clip or S-clip to the end of each extension.

LoomLove.com
Video Tutorial

Follow the instructions on page 26 to place the seed beads on black bands and the oval beads on purple bands.

Variation
Dot to Dot Bracelet

For a bracelet with a playful twist, we paired oval polka dot beads and Japanese glass seed beads in black with deep purple and black bands. To recreate this look, use the supplies listed below and follow the instructions on the preceding pages. Follow the instructions on page 26 to place the seed beads on black bands and the oval beads on purple bands.

Beads and Bands
» 50 solid bands in deep purple
» 30 solid bands in black
» I2 flat oval glass beads in black with iridescent dots (Halcraft's Bead Gallery Jet Glass Luster beads)
» 24 Japanese glass seed beads in black luster

Beaded Fishtail Bracelet

The Fishtail is another classic, and it's a perfect bracelet for beginners. Add beads, and you have an easy, stunning design that takes only minutes to make. Smaller beads work best for this bracelet style. We used small crystals. You can also use a Beaded Fishtail as a handle for the Cute Coin Purse (see page 132).

Level of Difficulty

» Easy

What You'll Need

» 75 solid bands in white

» 24 round faceted glass beads in clear (dismantled dollar store bracelet)

» 1 C-clip or S-clip

» 1 loom

» 1 hook

Loom Configuration

This bracelet is made using any two pegs on an outside row of the loom.

Banding the Beads

Following the instructions on page 26, place all the beads on the white bands.

MAKING THE BRACELET

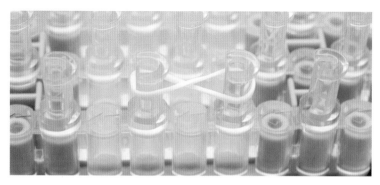

1. Place a single band in a figure eight shape on two pegs anywhere along an outside row of the loom.

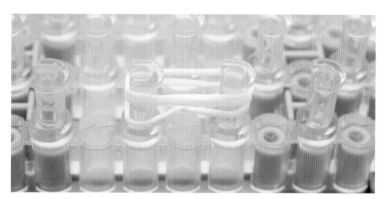

2. Place two more bands straight across on the same two pegs, over the figure eight band.

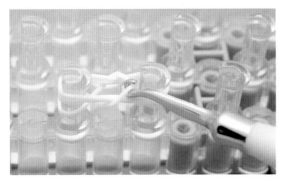

3. Hook the figure eight band from the outer right side and bring it over the right-hand peg to the center.

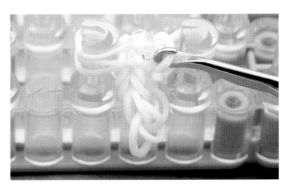

5. Continue this pattern, adding a beaded band and then a plain band, alternating between beaded and plain bands until the bracelet is long enough to fit around your wrist.

4. Repeat step 3 on the left side. Push the bands down on the pegs. Repeat steps 1 through 3, adding six more bands straight across the two pegs and looping the bottom band over the top one to the center each time.

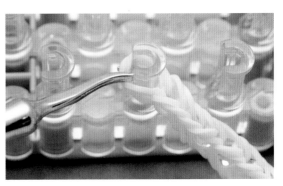

6. Bring both bands on the right peg to the left peg. Add a C-clip or S-clip and remove your bracelet from the loom.

LoomLove.com
Video Tutorial

Beaded Fishtail Dangles

These earrings are a cinch to make. We used Persian bands and tribal-style silver beads, closing off the earring with a silver split ring.

Level of Difficulty
» Easy

What You'll Need
» 30 Persian bands in yellow
» 10 small silver tribal-style beads (Halcraft Bead Gallery)
» 2 slip rings
» 2 French hook earring wires
» 1 loom
» 1 hook

Loom Configuration
These earrings are made using any two pegs on an outside row of the loom.

Banding the Beads
Following the instructions on page 26, place all the beads on the Persian bands.

MAKING THE EARRINGS

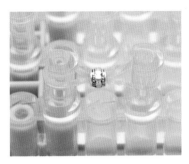

1. Place a beaded band on two pegs anywhere along an outside row of the loom.

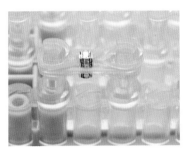

2. Place a plain band over the beaded band and then place a beaded band over the plain one.

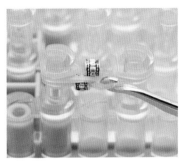

3. Hook the bottom beaded band from the outer right side and bring it over the right peg to the center. Repeat on the left side. Place another plain band over the previous bands and hook the bottom band over it.

4. Continue this pattern, alternating beaded and plain bands, until you've placed your last beaded band.

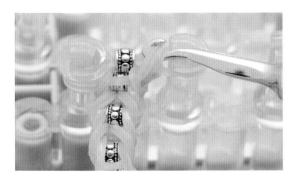

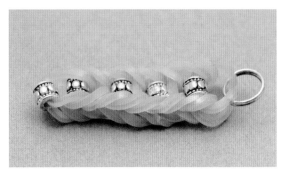

5. For the last beaded band, bring both bottom bands up and over the pegs and to the center, instead of just one.

7. Thread a slip ring through both loops.

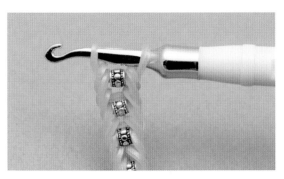

8. Add an earring wire to the slip ring. Repeat steps I through 8 to create a second earring.

6. Remove the earring from the loom by placing the top loops on your hook.

LoomLove.com
Video Tutorial

Shimmer Bracelet

This stunning design looks awesome with glass faceted beads in multiple colors. We used twelve beads to create the sample; you may need as many as thirteen or as few as nine, depending on your wrist size.

PLACING THE BANDS AND BEADS

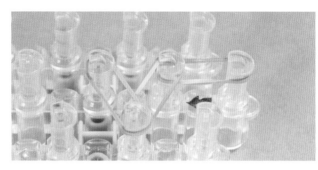

1. Position the double loom so the red arrow is pointing away from you. Place a gold band on peg 2 and stretch it up to peg 5. Place a gold band from peg 5 to peg 4 and another from peg 4 to peg 8. Place another gold band from peg 8 to 11. Repeat the pattern, peg 11 to 10, 10 to 14, 14 to 17, and so on, until you have as many points (pegs 4 and 10 make up the points) as you have beaded bands. (In this case, there are 12.) End with a vertical band from peg 74 to 77. This step is shown in illustration A.

A

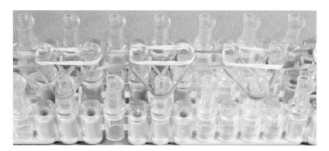

2. Place a teal cap band from peg 5 to peg 8, alongside of your first point. Repeat this pattern at each point, peg 11 to 14, peg 17 to 20, and so on.

LOOPING THE BANDS

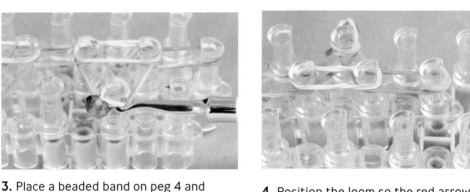

3. Place a beaded band on peg 4 and double it over on itself. Repeat on all of the other points you've made, on pegs 10, 16, and so on, ending on peg 70. Steps 2 and 3 are shown in illustration B.

4. Position the loom so the red arrow is pointing toward you. Place a teal cap band on peg 77.

5. Hook the gold band just below the cap band on peg 77. Pull it up and across to the peg directly above it, to peg 74.

B

C

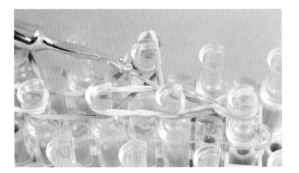

6. Hook the remaining gold band on peg 74. (It should be the band that's looped onto peg 70.) Pull it up and over to peg 70. Hook the bottom gold band on peg 70 and pull it up and over to peg 71. Repeat this pattern to the top of the loom. Steps 4 through 6 are shown in illustration C.

8. Add a C-clip or S-clip and remove your bracelet from the loom by releasing the beaded bands first.

7. Hook your final band from peg 5 to 2 and stretch both loops over to peg 3.

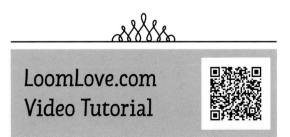

LoomLove.com
Video Tutorial

Jane Austen Bracelet

This elegant bracelet is one of our favorites. We used faceted glass beads and seed beads to make it sparkle.

Level of Difficulty
» Intermediate

What You'll Need
» 34 clear bands
» 32 bands in light purple
» 32 bands in violet
» 16 bands in dark purple
» 16 glass seed beads in clear (Darice Japanese Seed Beads)
» 16 large round faceted glass beads in smoky gray (dismantled dollar store bracelet)
» 1 C-clip or S-clip
» 2 looms
» 1 hook

Loom Configuration
Rectangular/even, double, with the right-hand verticle row removed

Banding the Beads
Following the instructions on page 26, place all of the beads on the clear bands.

PLACING THE BANDS AND BEADS

1. Position the loom so the red arrow is pointing away from you. Place your first beaded band (with a seed bead) from peg 1 to 3.

2. Place a second band (with a large faceted bead) from peg 3 to 5. Repeat this pattern, alternating between seed beads and faceted beads, until you've placed 16 beaded bands along the left-hand row, ending on peg 33.

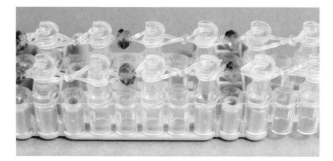

3. Repeat the pattern with the remaining beaded bands on the other row, from peg 2 to 4, 4 to 6, and so on, ending on peg 34. Steps 1 through 3 are shown in illustration A.

A

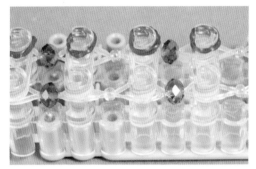

4. Place a light purple band from peg 3 to 4 and then place a violet band from peg 3 to 4. Continue up the loom, placing one band of each color from peg 5 to 6, 7 to 8, and so on until you reach the second-to-last pegs, peg 31 to 32.

5. Place a dark purple cap band on peg 4, then peg 6, and peg 8. Continue this pattern until you reach peg 32, the peg with your last double color bands. Place a clear cap band on peg 33 and another on peg 34. Steps 4 and 5 are shown in illustration B.

LOOPING THE BANDS

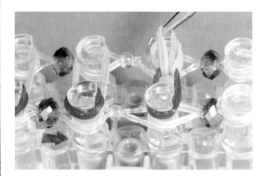

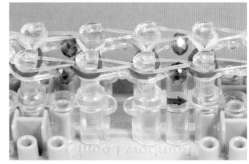

6. Reposition the loom so the red arrow is pointing toward you. Hook the two colored bands on peg 32 below the cap band and pull them up and across to peg 31. Continue by looping the two colored bands on peg 30 across to 29, and 28 to 27, and so on, until you reach the top of the loom. This step is shown in illustration C.

8. Repeat this looping pattern on the other row. Steps 7 and 8 are shown in illustration D.

9. Hook both clear bands on peg 2 and bring them over to peg 1.

7. Hook the clear beaded band below the cap band on peg 34 and bring it up and over to peg 32. Continue by hooking the bottom clear beaded band on peg 32 and bringing it up and over to peg 30. Repeat this pattern to the top of the loom.

D

10. Use your hook to thread through all of the bands on peg I. Place a single clear band on the hook and pull it through and around all the bands on that peg. Holding onto that new clear band, you can now remove your bracelet from the loom. Add a C-clip or S-clip to both ends of the bracelet.

Variation

Mansfield Park Bracelet

We went with shades of green for this lush version of the Jane Austen Bracelet. Use the supplies listed below and follow the instructions on the preceding pages.

Beads and Bands

» 34 clear bands

» 32 solid bands in yellow-green

» 32 solid bands in bright green

» 16 solid bands in blue-green

» 16 large round faceted glass beads in green

» 8 glass seed beads in clear

» 8 glass seed beads in matte green

LoomLove.com
Video Tutorial

Beaded Ladder Bracelet

If you're a seasoned loomer, you'll know that the Ladder design is a classic. When beads are added, it takes on an entirely different look. We paired round beads and jelly bands for this design.

PLACING THE BANDS AND BEADS

1. Position the loom so the arrow is pointing away from you. Place your first aqua band from peg 2 to 1. Place another aqua band from peg 1 to 4 and then continue along that row, placing a band from peg 4 to 7, 7 to 10, and so on, until you reach peg 34.

2. Place a band from peg 34 to 38.

3. Place a band from peg 2 to 3 and then continue along that row, placing bands from peg 3 to 6, 6 to 9, and so on, until you reach peg 36. Place a band from peg 36 to 38.

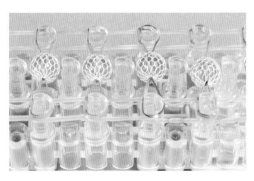

4. Place your first beaded band from peg 4 to 6 and then place the second beaded band from peg 7 to 9. Keep working along the loom in this same pattern until you place your last beaded band from peg 3I to 33. Steps I through 4 are shown in illustration A.

6. Hook the first band below the cap band (looped around peg 36), and bring it up and over to peg 36.

LOOPING THE BANDS

7. Hook the remaining band below the cap band on peg 38 and bring it up and across to peg 34.

5. Add a cap band to peg 38. Reposition the loom so the arrow is pointing toward you.

A

B

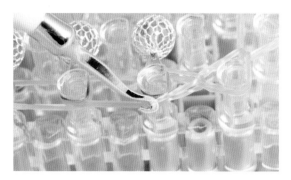

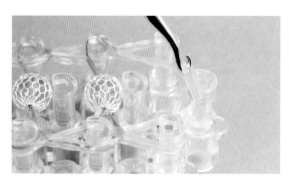

8. Hook the bottom band on peg 36 and stretch it vertically to peg 33. Repeat this pattern along that row by bringing the bottom band on peg 33 to 30, and so on, until you reach the last peg. When you get to peg 3, hook the bottom band up and over to peg 2. Repeat the same pattern along the other row by bringing the bottom band up and placing it vertically on the peg above. When you get to the last peg, bring the bottom band on peg I to peg 2. Steps 5 through 8 are shown in illustration B.

10. Pull the band to loop through all of the bands on peg 2. Holding onto the new band, you can now remove your bracelet from the loom. Following the instructions on page I9, create an extension for your bracelet so it fits around your wrist. We added a five-band extension to our design; you may need to add more bands. Add your C-clip or S-clip to the end of the extension.

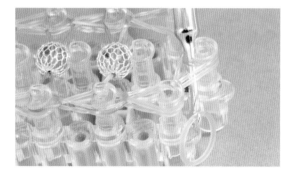

9. Use your hook to thread through all of the bands on peg 2 and place a single band on the hook.

LoomLove.com
Video Tutorial

Spring Bouquet Bracelet

Glitter bands give an added sparkle to this dazzling beaded design. Clear, square beads set into the pattern make this bracelet a knockout.

Level of Difficulty

» Intermediate

What You'll Need

» 45 sparkle bands in pink
» 30 sparkle bands in bright green
» 7 square glass faceted beads (Halcraft Bead Gallery)
» 1 C-clip or S-clip
» 2 looms
» 1 hook

Loom Configuration

Rectangular/even, double

Banding the Beads

Following the instructions on page 26, place four of the beads on the pink bands and three on the green bands.

PLACING THE BANDS AND BEADS

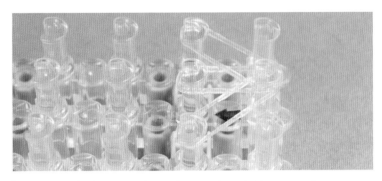

1. Position the loom so the red arrow is pointing away from you. Place your first pink band from peg 2 to peg 4. Place a second band from peg 2 to peg 5 and a third from peg 2 to peg 6.

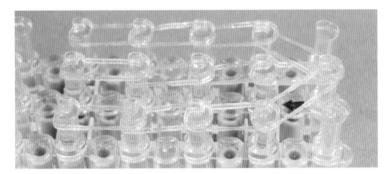

2. Place pink bands from peg 4 to peg 7, 7 to 10, and 10 to 13. Repeat this same pattern along the center row, starting on peg 5 to peg 14, then along the right row, from peg 6 to peg 15.

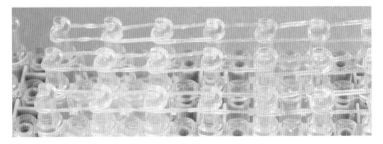

3. Repeat this same pattern by placing green bands along all three rows, starting on pegs 13, 14, and 15 ending on pegs 22, 23, and 24.

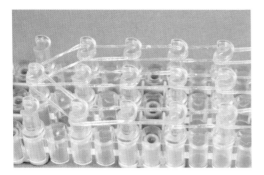

4. Repeat with another set of pink bands, from pegs 22, 23, and 24 to pegs 31, 32, and 33. Continue this pattern, alternating green and pink bands four more times, for a total of seven groupings. To finish, add a pink band from peg 67 to 71, 68 to 71, and 69 to 71. Steps 1 through 4 are shown in illustration A.

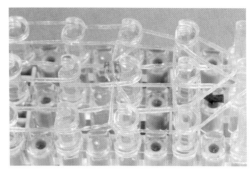

6. Place a beaded band with the same color bead as the bands in the grouping across from peg 7 to peg 9. The bead should rest in front of the peg in the middle. Place a second same color cap band from peg 10 to peg 12.

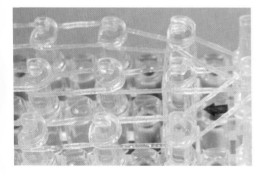

5. Make a cap band using the same color as the bands in the grouping by twisting it into a figure eight and doubling the band over itself. Stretch the double band across from peg 4 to peg 6.

7. Continue this pattern for each grouping, using bands and beads that match the color of the grouping.

8. Skip pegs 67, 68, and 69 and add a cap band to peg 71. Steps 5 through 8 are shown in illustration B.

A

B

LOOPING THE BANDS

9. Reposition the loom so the arrow is pointing toward you. On peg 71, use your hook to pull back the cap band. Hook the first band and stretch it back to peg 69.

10. Again, use the hook to pull back the cap band on peg 71. Hook the next band and stretch it back to peg 68. Repeat with the last band on peg 71 and stretch it back to peg 67.

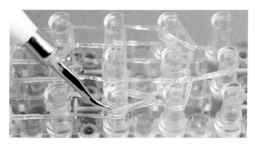

11. Hook the bottom band on peg 69 and bring it straight up to peg 66. Repeat from peg 66 to 63 and then continue along that row to peg 6. At peg 6, loop the band up to peg 2. Repeat this vertical pattern along the center row, from peg 68 to peg 5, and the right row, from peg 67 to peg 4. On pegs 5 and 4, bring the last bands up to peg 2. Steps 9 through 11 are shown in illustration C.

12. Use your hook to thread through all the bands on peg 2. Hook a single band to pull through to loop around all the bands on that peg. Slide the new band up and onto the grip of the hook and carefully remove the bracelet from the loom. Attach your C-clip or S-clip to the cap band on one end and the new band on the opposite end.

LoomLove.com
Video Tutorial

Beadazzled Bracelet

We're completely smitten with the Beadazzled design. We think it looks amazing with round faceted beads combined with white and bright blue bands.

Level of Difficulty
» Easy

What You'll Need
» 50 solid bands in white
» 45 solid bands in bright blue
» 21 round faceted glass beads in various colors (Halcraft's Bead Gallery Glass beads)
» 1 C-clip or S-clip
» 1 loom
» 1 hook

Loom Configuration
Offset/staggered

Banding the Beads
Following the instructions on page 26, place all of the beads on the bright blue bands.

PLACING THE BANDS AND BEADS

1. Position the loom so the arrow is pointing away from you. Place your first white band on peg 2 and stretch it up and across to peg 1. Place a second white band on peg 1 and stretch it to peg 4.

2. Continue by placing a band from peg 4 to 7, then 7 to 10, and so on, and working your way along the left-hand row up to peg 31.

3. Place a band from peg 2 to peg 5. Continue to add bands vertically along the center row to peg 32. Place your last white band from peg 32 to peg 31. Steps 1 through 3 are shown in illustration A.

4. Start adding beaded bands by placing the first band from peg 2 to peg 1 and then place a second band from peg 1 to peg 5. Continue in a zigzag pattern and finish with a beaded band from peg 32 to peg 31. This step is shown in illustration B.

LOOPING THE BANDS

5. Reposition the loom so the arrow is pointing toward you. Make a cap band by twisting a single white band over on itself and place it on peg 31.

6. Hook the white band just below the cap band on peg 31 and stretch it across to peg 32.

7. Hook the bottom white band on peg 31 and stretch it vertically to peg 28.

A

B

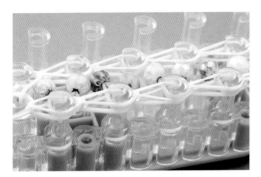

8. Continue this pattern, first along the left-hand row, hooking the bottom white band from peg 32 to peg 29, then 29 to 26, and so on, all the way to peg 2. Repeat along the other row by looping the bottom white band from peg 28 to 25, 25 to 22, and so on. When you get to peg 1, stretch it across to peg 2. Steps 5 through 8 are shown in illustration C.

C

9. Hook the remaining blue band on peg 31 and stretch it to peg 32.

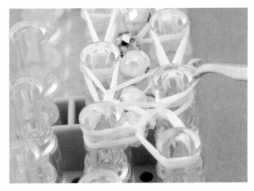

10. Hook the bottom blue band from peg 32 (this should be the band that holds the next bead in the zigzag pattern) and stretch it to peg 28.

11. Continue with this zigzag pattern, hooking beaded bands from peg 28 to 29, 29 to 25, and so on. Steps 9 though 11 are shown in illustration D.

D

12. Thread your hook through all of the bands on peg 2 and place a single white band on the hook.

13. Pull the single white band through all of the bands on the hook. Holding onto that new white band, you can now remove your bracelet from the loom. Attach a C-clip or S-clip to the cap band on one end and the new white band on the opposite end.

LoomLove.com
Video Tutorial

Gem Flower Bracelet

The Gem Flower was inspired by Made by Mommy's Beaded Starburst Flower bracelet. This gorgeous design works best with round beads that are less than 8 mm in diameter.

Level of Difficulty
» Intermediate

What You'll Need
» 75 clear bands
» 39 round faceted glass beads in various colors (Halcraft Bead Gallery)
» 1 C-clip or S-clip
» 2 looms
» 1 hook

Loom Configuration
Offset/staggered, double

Banding the Beads
Following the instructions on page 26, place all the beads on the clear bands.

PLACING THE BANDS AND BEADS

I. Position the loom so the arrow is pointing away from you. Place your first clear band from peg 2 to peg I, and a second from peg 2 to peg 3.

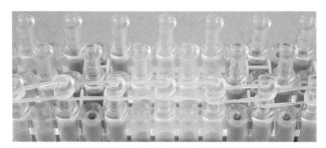

2. Place a clear band from peg I to peg 4, then 4 to 7. Continue working vertically along the left-hand row until you've placed I3 clear bands.

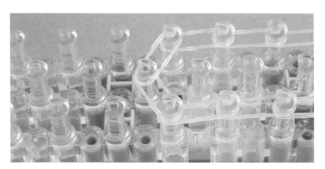

3. Repeat this vertical pattern on the right-hand row by placing a band from peg 3 to peg 6, then 6 to 9, and so on, until you've placed I3 clear bands. Place clear bands from peg 40 to peg 44 and peg 42 to peg 44. Steps I through 3 are shown in illustration A.

A

B

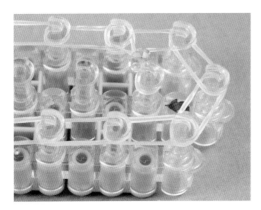

4. Place a beaded band from peg 5 to peg 6.

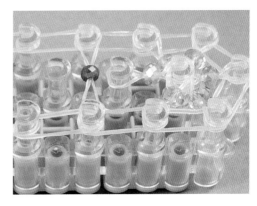

6. Place a beaded spacer band from peg 7 to peg 9.

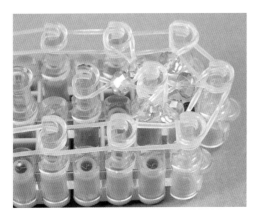

5. Working in a clockwise rotation, place beaded bands from peg 5 to peg 3, 5 to 2, 5 to l, 5 to 4, and 5 to 8.

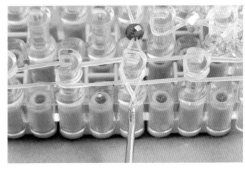

7. Hook the loop from peg 7 and twist it over on itself and back over peg 7. Repeat with the loop on peg 9.

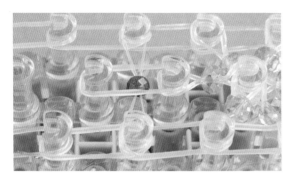

8. Place a clear band from peg 8 to peg 11.

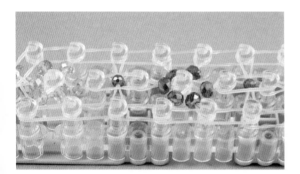

9. Make a second flower by placing beaded bands in the same clockwise rotation shown in steps 4 and 5 with the center on peg 14. Repeat steps 6 and 7 with a beaded spacer band from peg 16 to 18, twisting both sides as before and adding a single vertical band. Continue the patterns for flowers, spacer bands, and vertical single bands up the loom until you've placed your final flower with a center at peg 41. Steps 4 through 9 are shown in illustration B.

LOOPING THE BANDS

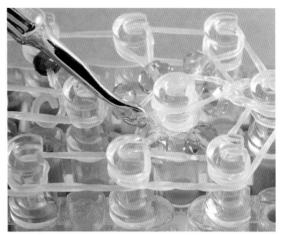

10. Reposition the loom so the arrow is pointing toward you. Place cap bands at the center of each flower and on peg 44. Hook the beaded band just below the cap band on peg 44 and bring it forward to the center of the flower on peg 41.

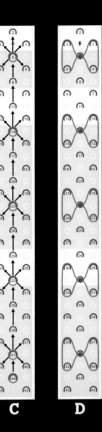

C

D

E

11. Hook the second beaded band on peg 41 (this should be the band that has a bead between peg 41 and 40) and bring it up and over to peg 40. Continue in a counterclockwise pattern by grabbing the top beaded band on peg 41 and bringing it up and over to the outer peg that it's connected to.

12. Begin the pattern again by hooking the bottom band on peg 38 and bringing it up and over to peg 35. Hook the bottom beaded band on peg 35 and bring it up and over to peg 32. Repeat the flower looping pattern by bringing the top beaded band to its corresponding outer peg, working in a counterclockwise pattern. Repeat this sequence to the top of the loom. Steps 11 and 12 are shown in illustration C.

I3. To add your flower center, place one loop on the beaded band from peg 42 to peg 39 and the loop on the other side of the beaded band from peg 40 to peg 37. Repeat this pattern to add centers to all flowers on the loom. (This is shown in illustration D.) Hook the top clear band under the cap band on peg 44 and bring it up and over to peg 40 and the bottom clear band on peg 44 to peg 42. Hook the bottom clear band on peg 42 and bring it up and over to peg 39, then peg 39 to 36, and so on, until you reach the top of the loom. Repeat this pattern on the other side of the loom. (This is shown in illustration E.) Thread the hook through all of the bands on peg 2 and hook a single band to pull through and loop around all the bands on that peg. Holding onto that new band, you can now remove your bracelet from the loom. Add a C-clip or S-clip to both ends of the bracelet. You may need to pull the beaded bands in the center of each flower up and towards the surface.

LoomLove.com Video Tutorial

Variation
Gem Session Bracelet

To change up the look of the Gem Flower design, we used black bands and blue beads paired with beads in shades of gold and copper. Use the supplies listed below and follow the instructions on the preceding pages.

Beads and Bands
» 75 black bands
» 5 copper seed beads (Darice Japanese Seed Beads)
» 4 iridescent faceted glass beads (Halcraft Bead Gallery Beads)
» 6 faceted metallic glass beads (Halcraft Bead Gallery Beads)
» I2 round turquoise glass beads (dismantled dollar store bracelet)
» I2 round blue glass beads (dismantled dollar store bracelet)

Gem Flower Hairclip

The Gem Flower Hairclip was inspired by Made by Mommy's Beaded Flower Charm design. We used pale pink bands, round crystal beads, and a single gold bead for the center. You'll need a barrette or alligator hairclip for this design.

Level of Difficulty

» Easy

What You'll Need

» 25 sparkle bands in pale pink

» 6 large round faceted glass beads with iridescent stripes in various colors (Halcraft Bead Gallery)

» I small round faceted glass bead in gold (Halcraft Bead Gallery)

» I barrette or alligator hairclip

» I loom

» I hook

Loom Configuration

Offset/staggered

Banding the Beads

Following the instructions on page 26, place all of the beads on the sparkle bands.

MAKING THE HAIRCLIP

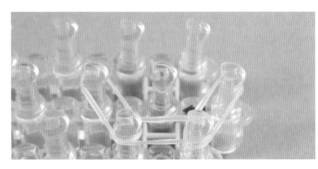

I. Position the loom with the arrow facing away from you. Place your first band from peg 2 to peg I, a second from peg I to peg 4, and a third from peg 4 to peg 8.

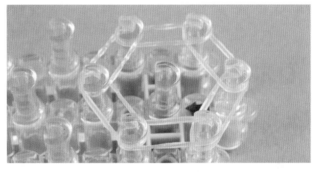

2. Repeat on the other side by placing bands from peg 2 to peg 3, from peg 3 to peg 6, and from peg 6 to peg 8.

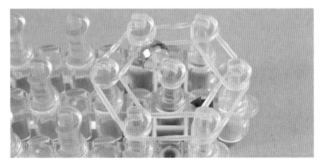

3. Place a beaded band from peg 5 to peg 6 and, working in a clockwise rotation, place beaded bands from peg 5 to 3, 5 to 2, 5 to I, 5 to 4, and 5 to 8. Steps I through 3 are shown in illustration A.

B

C

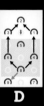

D

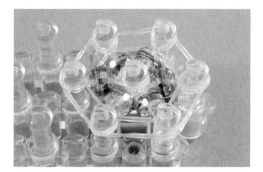

4. Reposition your loom so the arrow is pointing toward you. Place a cap band on the center of the flower, on peg 5.

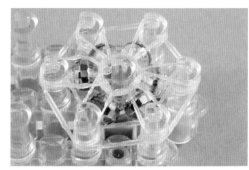

6. Add a cap band to peg 8.

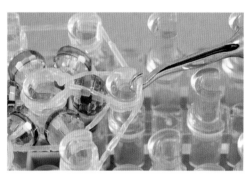

5. Hook the beaded band just below the cap band on peg 5 and bring it up and over to itself on peg 8. Hook the next beaded band on peg 5 and bring it up and over to itself on peg 4. Working counterclockwise, continue this pattern for each beaded band of the flower. Steps 4 and 5 are shown in illustration B.

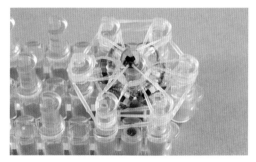

7. To add your flower center, place one loop on the gold beaded band from peg I to peg 4 and the loop on the other side of the beaded band from peg 3 to peg 6. (This step is shown in illustration C.) Hook the top single band under the cap band and beaded bands on peg 8 and bring it up and over to peg 6. Hook the bottom single band on peg 8 and bring it up and over to peg 4. Hook the bottom single band on peg 6 and bring it up and across to peg 3. Hook the bottom single band on peg 3 and bring up and across to peg 2. Repeat this pattern on the other side. Thread your hook through all the bands on peg 8 and hook a single band to pull through and loop around all the bands on that peg. Place this newly added loop onto peg 9. This step is shown in illustration D.

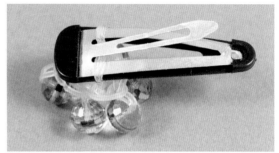

8. Hook the bottom loop on peg 9 up and over the top to create a slip knot and pull. Repeat by adding a new band through all of the bands on peg 2 and create a slip knot by bringing the bottom loop over the top and pulling to tighten the knot. You can now remove the flower from the loom.

9. Double both slip knot loops as you would with a cap band. Place the bands through an open barrette or alligator hairclip and slowly slide it to the top.

LoomLove.com
Video Tutorial

Gem Flower Key Chain

This awesome project combines motifs from the Gem Flower and Beaded Ladder bracelets (see pages 66 and 53). We used seed beads and round crystal beads.

Level of Difficulty
» Easy

What You'll Need
» 40 solid bands in purple

» 25 solid bands in yellow-orange

» 12 large round faceted glass beads in pale purple (dismantled dollar store bracelet)

» 17 glass seed beads in orange (Darice Japanese Seed Beads)

» 1 key chain loop

» 1 loom

» 2 hooks

Loom Configuration
Offset/staggered

Banding the Beads
Following the instructions on page 26, place six of the large beads on the purple bands, two large beads each on three yellow-orange bands, one orange seed bead on a yellow-orange band, and four seed beads each on four yellow-orange bands.

MAKING THE KEY CHAIN

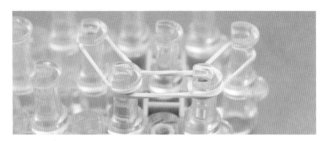

1. Position the loom so the arrow is pointing away from you. Place your first purple band from peg 2 to peg 1, a second from 1 to 4, and a third from 4 to 8.

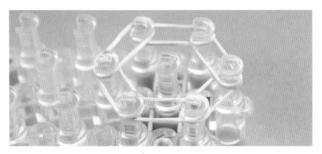

2. Repeat on the other side by placing purple bands from peg 2 to peg 3, 3 to 6, and 6 to 8.

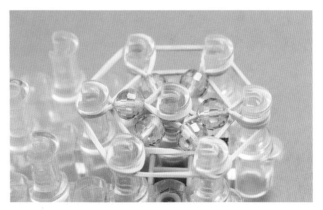

3. Place a round beaded band from peg 5 to peg 6. Working in a clockwise rotation, place beaded bands from peg 5 to peg 3, 5 to 2, 5 to 1, 5 to 4, and 5 to 8. Steps 1 through 3 are shown in illustration A.

B

C

D

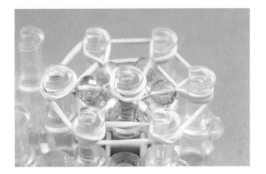

4. Reposition the loom so the arrow is pointing toward you. Place a cap band on the center of the flower (on peg 5) and a second cap band on peg 8.

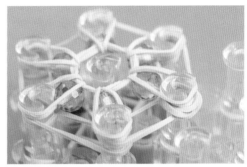

6. Hook the next beaded band on peg 5 and bring it up and over to itself on peg 4. Working counterclockwise, continue this pattern for each beaded band of the flower. Steps 5 and 6 are shown in illustration B.

5. Hook the beaded band just below the cap band on peg 5 and bring it up and over to itself on peg 8.

7. To add your flower center, place one loop from a seed beaded band from peg I to peg 4 and the loop on the other side of the beaded band from peg 3 to peg 6. This step is shown in illustration C.

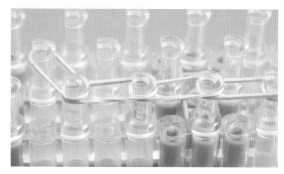

8. Hook the top single band under the cap band and beaded bands on peg 5 and bring it up and over to peg 6. Grab the bottom single band on peg 5 and bring it up and over to peg 4. Hook the bottom single band on peg 6 and bring it up and over to peg 3. Grab the bottom single band on peg 3 and bring it up and over to peg 2. Repeat this pattern on the other side. This step is shown in illustration D.

10. Reposition the loom so the arrow is facing away from you. Place your first purple band from peg 2 to peg 1, a second from 1 to 4, and a third from 4 to 7. Place bands along the left-hand row until you've placed a band from peg 16 to peg 19. Place a final band from peg 19 to peg 23.

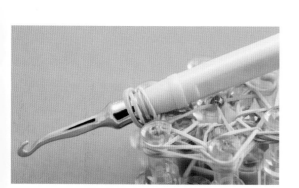

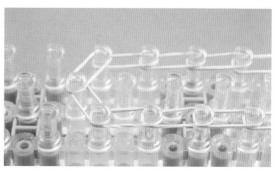

9. Thread your hook through all of the bands on peg 2. Hook two bands to pull through and loop around all of the bands on that peg. Pull the two new bands onto the gripper of your hook. Remove the flower from the loom and set it aside, leaving the flower on the hook.

11. Repeat to place bands vertically along the right-hand row, and then a final band from peg 21 to peg 23.

E

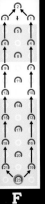

F

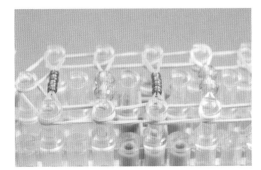

12. Place an orange band with four seed beads from peg I to peg 3 and a purple band with two round beads from peg 4 to peg 6. Repeat this pattern until you've placed your final band from peg 19 to peg 2I. Steps 10 through 12 are shown in illustration E.

13. Reposition the loom so that the arrow is pointing toward you. Attach your flower by placing all of the loops on your hook on peg 23.

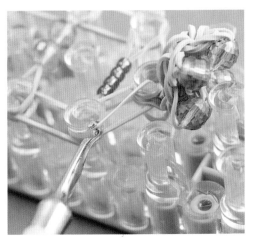

14. Use your hook to push back all the bands from the flower on peg 23. Hook the top single band and bring it up and over to itself on peg 2I. Hook the second single band under all the flower bands on peg 23 and bring it up and over to peg 19.

15. Loop the bands vertically by hooking the bottom band on peg 2I and bringing it up and to peg 18, then from 18 to 15, and so on, until you reach the top of the loom and loop peg 3 to peg 2. Repeat this step along the other row. Steps 14 and 15 are shown in illustration F.

16. Thread your hook through all of the bands on peg 2 and then hook a single band to pull through and loop around all the bands on that peg. Holding onto that new band, you can now remove your key chain from the loom.

17. Attach both loops onto a key chain loop.

LoomLove.com
Video Tutorial

Crystal Wave Bracelet

This easy bracelet has a wave-like pattern. We used clear bands to highlight this pattern, along with pastel bands, seed beads, and faceted glass beads.

Level of Difficulty

» Easy

What You'll Need

» 25 pastel bands in yellow

» 25 clear bands

» 7 large round faceted glass beads in yellow (dismantled dollar store bracelet)

» 13 glass seed beads in orange (Darice Japanese Seed Beads)

» 1 C-clip or S-clip

» 1 loom

» 1 hook

Loom Configuration

Offset/staggered

Banding the Beads

Following the instructions on page 26, place all of the beads on the yellow bands.

PLACING THE BANDS AND BEADS

1. Place your first round beaded band from peg 2 to peg 3. Place a seed beaded band from peg 3 to peg 5 and a third seed beaded band from peg 5 to 4.

2. Place a round beaded band from peg 4 to peg 8 and a seed beaded band from peg 8 to 9.

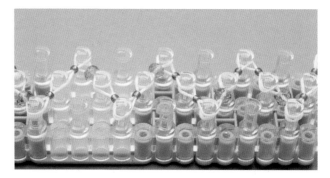

3. Continue this zigzag pattern of a round beaded band followed by two seed beaded bands for the length of the loom. End with a seed beaded band from peg 28 to peg 32. Steps 1 through 3 are shown in illustration A.

A

LOOPING THE BANDS

4. Place a clear band from peg 2 to peg I, a second from I to 5, and another from 5 to 6.

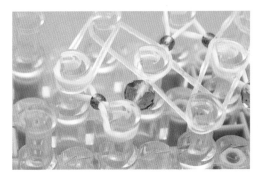

6. Reposition the loom so the red arrow is pointing toward you. Place a cap band on peg 32.

5. Continue this zigzag pattern until you place your last clear band from peg 30 to peg 32. Steps 4 and 5 are shown in illustration B.

7. Hook the top clear band under the cap band on peg 32 and bring it up and over to peg 30.

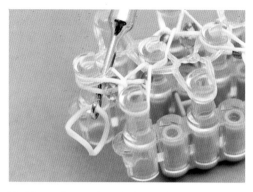

8. Hook the clear band on peg 30 and bring it up and over to peg 29. Continue looping the clear bands up and over to the next peg in the zigzag pattern until you reach the bottom of the loom. This step is shown in illustration C.

10. Thread your hook through all of the bands on peg 2. Pull a single band through and loop it around all the bands on that peg. Holding onto that new yellow band, you can now remove your bracelet from the loom. Add a C-clip or S-clip to both ends of the bracelet.

9. Hook the single beaded band on peg 32 and bring it up and over to peg 28. Continue looping the single beaded bands in the zigzag pattern until you reach the bottom of the loom. This step is shown in illustration D.

D

LoomLove.com
Video Tutorial

Starglow Bracelet

This fantastic design combines silver metallic bands with round silver beads and clear seed beads. Persian and pastel bands were also used.

Level of Difficulty
» Intermediate

What You'll Need
» 48 metallic bands in silver

» 24 Persian bands in gold/green

» 20 pastel bands in blue

» 24 large round metal beads in sparkling silver (Halcraft Bead Gallery)

» 24 small round glass beads in clear (Darice Japanese Seed Beads)

» 1 C-clip or S-clip

» 2 looms

» 1 hook

Loom Configuration
Offset/staggered, double

Banding the Beads
Following the instructions on page 26, place all of the beads on the metallic silver bands.

PLACING THE BANDS AND BEADS

I. Position the loom so the red arrow is pointing away from you. Place a silver beaded band from peg 2 to peg 1. Place a seed beaded band from peg 1 to peg 4, then a silver beaded band from peg 4 to 7, followed by a seed beaded band from peg 7 to 11.

2. Continue this pattern along the left row by adding a beaded band from peg 11 to 10, 10 to 13, 13 to 16, and 16 to 20, alternating silver and seed beads as you go. Continue until you place your last beaded band from peg 52 to 56.

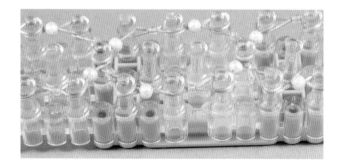

3. Repeat this pattern along the right-hand row, ending on peg 56. The configuration of beaded bands should create circle shapes. Steps 1 through 3 are shown in illustration A.

B

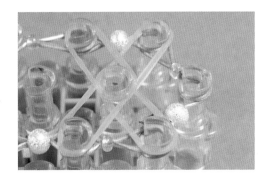

4. Place a gold/green band from peg I to peg 5, a second from 5 to 3, another from 4 to 5, and a fourth from 5 to 6. This will form an X at the bottom of the circle.

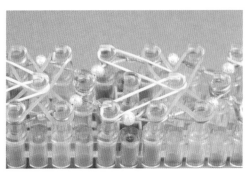

6. Repeat steps 4 and 5 to create a gold/green X and a blue V in the next circle. Continue this pattern until you reach your last circle of beaded bands. Add a silver cap band to peg 56. Steps 3 though 6 are shown in illustration B.

5. Place a blue band from peg 5 to peg 7 and a second from 5 to 9 to form a V at the top of the circle.

Bracelet Length

Note that ending the pattern on peg 56 creates a kid's-length bracelet. Depending on the size of your wrist, you may want to add another circle of beaded bands; if you prefer to make the bracelet following these instructions, you may need to add an extension after the bracelet is complete.

LOOPING THE BANDS

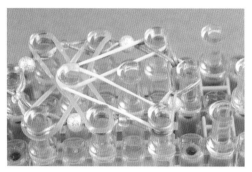

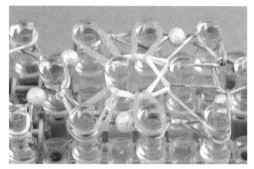

7. Reposition the loom so the red arrow is pointing toward you. Note in illustration C that the bands and beads are looped in two stages: the inner bands first (shown in black arrows), then the outer, beaded bands (shown in blue). Start by hooking the silver band just below the cap band on peg 56 and bring it up and over to peg 54. Grab the second silver band on peg 56 and bring it up and over to peg 52.

9. Hook the top gold/green band on peg 50 and loop it up and over on itself to peg 51. Continue in a counterclockwise pattern, looping the next band on peg 50 and bringing it up and over on itself to peg 49, and so on, until you've looped all the gold/green bands.

C

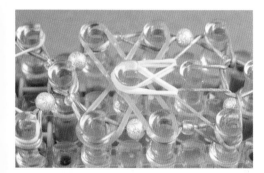

8. Hook the blue band on peg 54 and bring it up and over to peg 50. Repeat on the other side by looping the blue band on peg 52 up and over to peg 50.

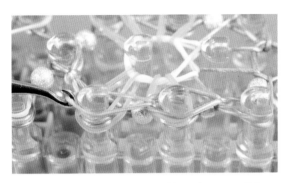

10. Hook the bottom beaded band on peg 54 and bring it up and over to peg 51. Repeat for peg 51 to 48, then 48 to 47.

12. Thread your hook through all of the bands on peg 2. Pull a single band through and loop it around all the bands on that peg. Holding onto that band, remove your bracelet from the loom. Add a C-clip or S-clip to both ends of the bracelet.

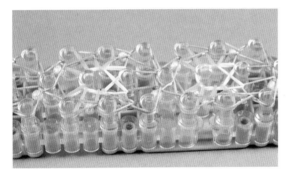

11. Starting with peg 47, repeat steps 7 though 10 to continue the established pattern, looping the blue bands first, then gold-green bands, then the beaded band, until you reach the end of the loom. See illustration C.

LoomLove.com
Video Tutorial

Illumine Bracelet

The Illumine bracelet looks great with alternating colored bands. We used faceted glass beads that match the colors of the bands.

Level of Difficulty
» Easy

What You'll Need
» 60 jelly bands in blue
» 60 solid bands in violet
» 6 round faceted glass beads in blue (Darice dismantled bracelet)
» 6 round faceted glass beads in purple (Darice dismantled bracelet)
» I C-clip or S-clip
» I loom
» I hook

Loom Configuration
Offset/staggered

Banding the Beads
Following the instructions on page 26, place the purple beads on the violet bands and the blue beads onto the blue bands.

PLACING THE BANDS AND BEADS

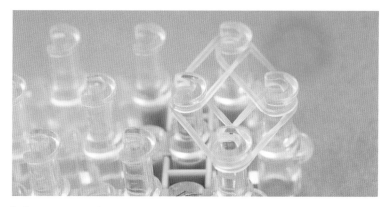

I. Position your loom so the red arrow is pointing away from you. Make a diamond shape by placing a blue band from peg 2 to peg I, a second from 2 to 3, a third from I to 5, and the last from 5 to 3.

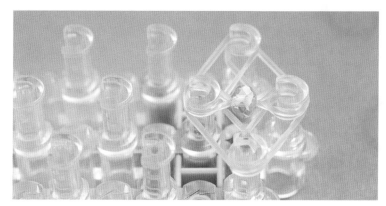

2. Place a matching blue beaded band from peg 5 to peg 2.

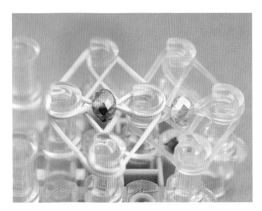

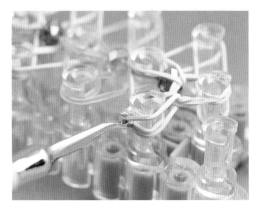

3. Starting at peg 5, repeat steps 1 and 2 to make a second diamond shape with purple bands and then add a matching beaded band from peg 5 to peg 8. Continue making diamonds, alternating colors and adding matching beaded bands, until you reach the top of the loom. (To make our design, you'll place your last purple beaded band from peg 35 to 38.) The remaining two pegs on either side will not have bands. Steps 1 through 3 are shown in illustration A.

5. Hook the new top band just below the cap band on peg 38 and bring it up and over to peg 36.

LOOPING THE BANDS

6. Hook the remaining band on peg 38 just below the cap band and bring it up and over to peg 34.

4. Reposition the loom so the red arrow is pointing toward you. Place a purple cap band on peg 38. Hook the top beaded band just below the cap band on peg 38 and bring it up and over to peg 35.

A

B

7. Hook the bottom band on peg 36 and bring it up and over to peg 35. Repeat to bring the bottom band on peg 34 to peg 35.

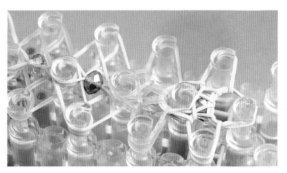

9. Hook the bottom band on peg 33 and bring it up and over to peg 32. Repeat on the other side by bringing the bottom band on peg 31 and bringing it over to peg 32. Repeat this looping pattern for each diamond shape until you reach the end of the loom. (Steps 4 though 9 are shown in illustration B.) Thread your hook through all the bands on peg 2. Pull through a single band and loop it around all the bands on that peg. Holding onto that new band, you can remove your bracelet from the loom. Add a C-clip or an S-clip to both ends of the bracelet.

8. Hook the top blue band below the purple bands on peg 35 (this should be the band connected to peg 32) and bring it up and over to peg 32. Hook the next blue band on peg 35 and bring it up and over to peg 33. Repeat to bring the last blue band on peg 35 to peg 31.

LoomLove.com
Video Tutorial

Beaded Lantern Bracelet

For this stunning design, we went for a modern, industrial look, using clear and silver bands along with large metallic mesh beads.

PLACING THE BANDS AND BEADS

1. Position your loom so the openings of the C-shaped pegs are facing away from you. Place two silver bands from peg 1 to peg 3, place two more bands from 3 to 5, and continue until you reach the top of the loom. Repeat this pattern on the other row. This step is shown in illustration A.

LOOPING THE BANDS AND ADDING THE BEADS

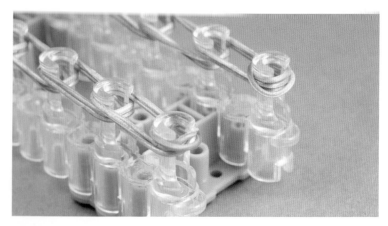

2. Turn the loom so the openings of the C-shaped pegs are now facing toward you. Place a cap band on peg 25 and peg 26.

3. Hook the bottom two bands below the cap band on peg 26 and bring them up and over to peg 24. Repeat with peg 25, bringing the bands up and over to peg 23.

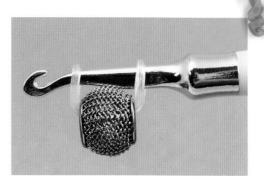

5. Place both loops of the band on the hook.

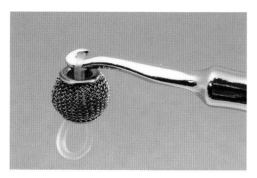

4. Place a large bead on your hook. Pull a single clear band through the bead hole.

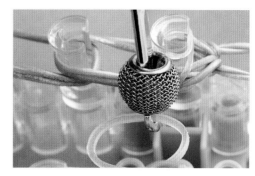

6. Place both loops on peg 23.

7. Place the hook through the center of the bead and pull through another single band. Place this band on peg 24.

9. Thread your hook through all the bands on peg 2 and loop two single bands through all the bands on that peg. Place the added loops on another hook (or on another placeholder, such as a pen, as shown).

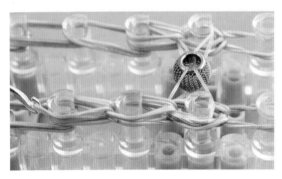

8. Hook the bottom two bands below the beaded band on peg 24 and bring them up and over to peg 22. Repeat with peg 23, bringing the bands up and over to peg 21. Repeat again, hooking the bottom two bands on peg 22 and bringing them up and over to peg 20, then again with peg 21, bringing the bands up and over to peg 19. Follow steps 4 through 7 to place a second bead on pegs 20 and 19. Continue this pattern, adding beads on every other set of pegs, along the length of the loom. Steps 2 though 8 are shown in illustration B.

10. Repeat for peg 1, this time leaving the added loops on the hook and then taking the loops from peg 2 from the placeholder and back on the hook. With all the loops on the hook, you can now remove the bracelet from the loom. Following the instructions on page 19, create an extension for your bracelet so it fits around your wrist. We added a double six-band extension to our design; you may need to add more bands to make your bracelet fit.

LoomLove.com
Video Tutorial

Sparkle Square Bracelet

Alternating colors with clear bands gives this bracelet its unique pattern. Glass seed beads add sparkle.

Level of Difficulty
» Easy

What You'll Need
» 35 clear bands

» 8 solid bands in orange

» 12 solid bands in blue

» 4 solid bands in purple

» 8 glass seed beads in orange (Darice Japanese Seed Beads)

» 12 glass seed beads in blue (Darice Japanese Seed Beads)

» 4 glass seed beads in purple (Darice Japanese Seed Beads)

» 1 C-clip or S-clip

» 2 looms

» 1 hook

Loom Configuration
Rectangular/even, double

Banding the Beads
Following the instructions on page 26, place two orange beads each on four orange bands, two blue beads each on six blue bands, and two purple beads each on two purple bands.

PLACING THE BANDS AND BEADS

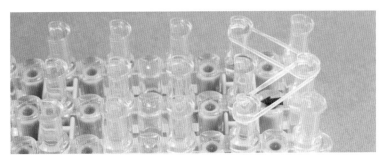

1. Position the loom so the red arrow is facing away from you. Add a clear band from peg 2 to peg 4. Add a second clear band from peg 2 to peg 6.

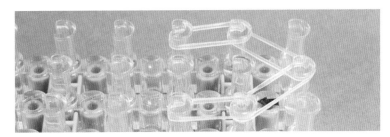

2. Place clear bands from peg 4 to peg 7 and 6 to 9.

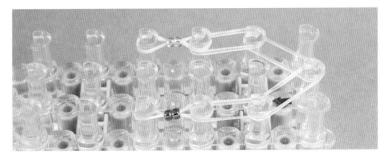

3. Place blue beaded bands from peg 7 to peg 10 and 9 to 12.

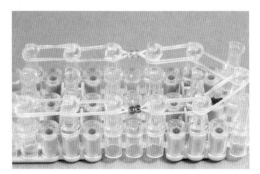

4. Place clear bands from peg 10 to peg 13 and 13 to 16 and from peg 12 to peg 15 and 15 to 18.

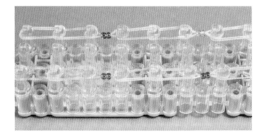

5. Place vertical orange beaded bands from peg 16 to peg 19 and 18 to 21. Continue the pattern, placing a clear band from peg 19 to peg 22 and 22 to 25 and then from peg 21 to 24 and 24 to 27.

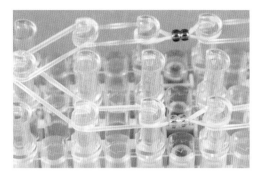

6. Continue the pattern by adding one purple beaded band followed by two clear bands on each side. Repeat the pattern, ending with blue beaded bands from peg 52 to peg 55 and 54 to 57. Place a clear band from peg 55 to peg 58, from 57 to 60, and then from 58 to 62 and 60 to 62. Steps 1 though 6 are shown in illustration A.

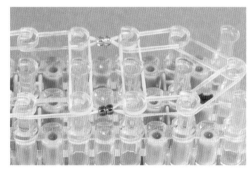

7. Place a single blue band around pegs 7, 8, and 9 and on pegs 10, 11, and 12. This should form a rectangle shape.

A

B

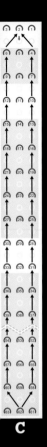

C

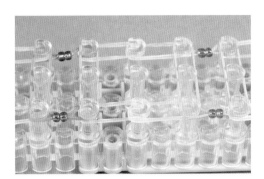

8. Repeat this pattern on either side of every beaded section, using the same color as the beaded bands. Add a clear cap band to peg 62. Steps 7 and 8 are shown in illustration B.

LOOPING THE BANDS

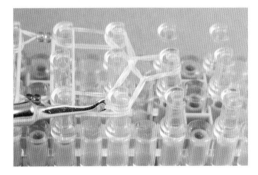

9. Reposition the loom so the red arrow is pointing toward you. Hook the clear band just below the cap band on peg 62 and bring it up and over to peg 58. Repeat by bringing the second clear band on peg 62 up and over to peg 60.

10. Grab the bottom clear band on peg 60 and bring it up and over vertically to peg 57. Continue to loop the bands, working toward the end of the loom, first on the left row, then on the right, by bringing the bottom band up to the peg above. When you reach peg 6 (on the left) and peg 4 (on the right), grab the bottom clear band and bring it up and over to peg 2. Steps 9 and 10 are shown in illustration C.

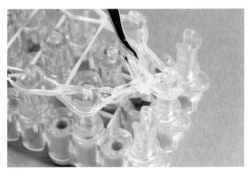

11. Thread your hook through all of the bands on peg 2 and pull through a single band to loop all the bands together. You can now remove your bracelet from the loom and attach a C-clip or S-clip.

LoomLove.com
Video Tutorial

Whirlwind Bracelet

The Whirlwind is one of our most elegant designs. With 89 beads, this bracelet is time-consuming but definitely worth the effort. A unique technique of twisting rubber bands—we used Persian and black bands—is used to create the spiral effect in the design.

Level of Difficulty
» Challenging

What You'll Need
» 55 solid bands in black
» 30 Persian bands in black/gold
» 80 glass seed beads in iridescent (Darice Japanese Seed Beads)
» 9 large round beads in iridescent (Halcraft Bead Gallery)
» 1 C-clip or S-clip
» 2 looms
» 1 hook

Loom Configuration
Offset/staggered, double

Banding the Beads
Following the instructions on page 26, place two seed beads each on black bands (for a total of forty bands) and place each of the nine large beads on a black band.

PLACING THE BANDS AND BEADS

1. Position your loom so the red arrow is pointing away from you. Place your first seed beaded band from peg 2 to peg 1.

2. Continue by placing seed beaded bands from peg 1 to peg 4, 4 to 7, and so on, until you've placed the final band from peg 55 to peg 58.

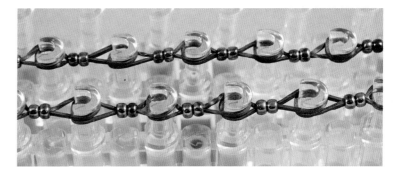

3. Place a seed beaded band from peg 2 to peg 5 and then continue vertically as you did on the other row, placing a final band from peg 56 to peg 59.

4. Place a seed beaded band from peg 59 to peg 58. Steps I through 4 are shown in illustration A.

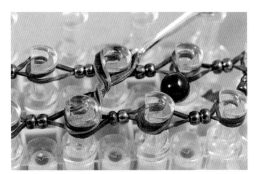

6. Place three single bands on peg 7. Use your hook to pull them away from the peg, twist two times, and then place them on peg 8.

5. Place a large beaded band from peg 4 to peg 5.

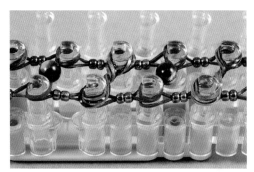

7. Repeat steps 5 and 6 in an alternating pattern, placing a large beaded band from peg 10 to peg II and three twisted bands from peg 13 to peg 14. Continue this pattern until your last twisted bands are placed from peg 55 to peg 56. Steps 5 through 7 are shown in illustration B.

A

B

LOOPING THE BANDS

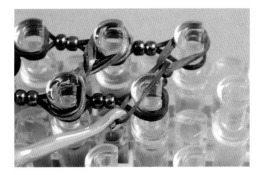

8. Reposition the loom so the red arrow is pointing toward you. Use a single black band to make a cap band on peg 58. Hook the top beaded band just under the cap band on peg 58 and bring it up and over to 59.

9. Work vertically up the loom by looping the bottom beaded band on peg 59 and bringing it forward to peg 56, then from peg 56 to peg 53, and so on, until you reach the top of the loom.

10. Repeat this pattern on the other row by looping the bottom beaded band from peg 58 to peg 55, then from peg 55 to peg 52, and so on, until you reach the top of the loom. Finish by looping from peg 2 to peg 1. (Steps 8 though 10 are shown in illustration C.) Thread your hook through all the bands on peg 2 and hook a single band through, looping it through all the bands on that peg. Holding onto that new band, you can remove your bracelet from the loom. Add a C-clip or S-clip to both ends of the bracelet.

C

LoomLove.com
Video Tutorial

Diamond Eyes Bracelet

Clear and pastel bands provide the perfect backdrop for alternating round and square glass beads in this stunning bracelet design.

Level of Difficulty

» Easy

What You'll Need

» 50 clear bands

» 20 solid bands in white

» 8 round faceted glass beads in iridescent (Halcraft Bead Gallery)

» 8 square faceted glass beads in iridescent (Halcraft Bead Gallery)

» 1 C-clip or S-clip

» 2 looms

» 1 hook

Loom Configuration

Rectangular/even, double

Banding the Beads

Following the instructions on page 26, place all of the beads on the clear bands.

PLACING THE BANDS AND BEADS

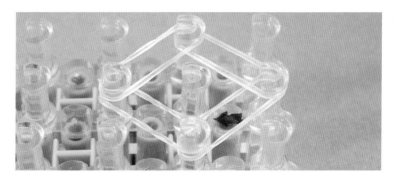

1. Position your loom so the red arrow is pointing away from you. Place your first clear band from peg 2 to peg 4, a second from 4 to 8, a third from 2 to 6, and the last from 6 to 8. This will form a diamond shape. This step is shown with green arrows in illustration A.

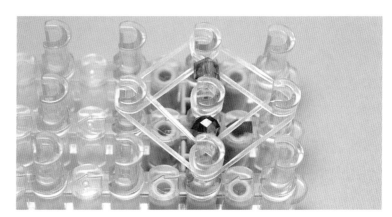

2. Place a round beaded band from peg 4 to peg 5 and a square beaded band from peg 5 to peg 6.

LOOPING THE BANDS

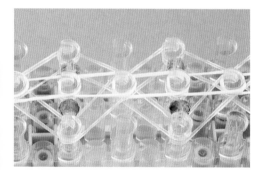

3. Place a white band from peg 2 to peg 5 and a second from 5 to 8. Steps 2 and 3 are shown with blue arrows in illustration A.

4. Repeat steps I through 3 to make a diamond shape, starting at peg 8 and adding 2 beaded bands (alternating round and square beads) and 2 white bands as before. Repeat this pattern until you have formed 8 diamond shapes. The entire sequence is shown in illustration A.

5. Reposition your loom so the red arrow is pointing toward you. Add a cap band to peg 50. Hook the top white band just below the cap band on peg 50 and bring it up and over to peg 47.

6. Hook the top white band on peg 47 and bring it up and over to peg 44.

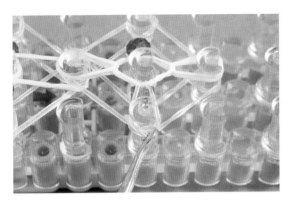

7. Hook the top clear beaded band on peg 47 and bring it up and over to peg 48. Grab the bottom clear beaded band on peg 47 and bring it up and over to peg 46. Steps 5 through 7 are shown with black arrows in illustration B.

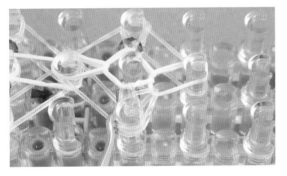

8. Hook the top clear band under the cap band on peg 50 and bring it over to peg 48. Hook the bottom clear band from peg 48 and bring it over to peg 44.

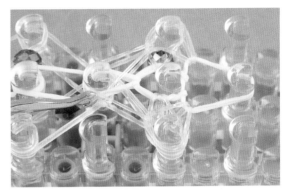

9. Grab the bottom clear band on peg 50 and bring it up and across to peg 46. Grab the bottom clear band on peg 46 and bring it up and across to peg 44. (The arrows for steps 7 through 9 are shown in blue in illustration B.) Continue this same pattern on all the diamond shapes, first bringing the white bands forward, then looping the beaded bands to the sides, and then bringing the clear bands on both sides forward, as shown in illustration B. Thread your hook through all of the bands on peg 2 and then pull a single band through and loop it around all the bands on that peg. Holding onto that new band, you can remove your bracelet from the loom. Add a C-clip or S-clip to both ends of the bracelet.

LoomLove.com
Video Tutorial

Beaded Rainbow Blossoms Bracelet

This bracelet is one of our most extravagant designs. We love how it looks, and we love how it feels. It's super comfortable to wear. We matched the color of the beads to the colors of the bands. Seed beads frame the edges of each of the five "flowers" that make up the bracelet, while faceted glass beads make the "petals" sparkle. With 180 beads, making this bracelet is time-consuming, but the result is magnificent!

What You'll Need

» 20 solid bands in pink

» 7 clear bands

» 19 solid bands each in gold, green, blue, and purple

» 6 round faceted glass beads each in pink, clear, green, blue, and purple (dismantled dollar store bracelet)

» 30 glass seed beads each in pink, gold, green, blue, and purple (Darice Japanese Seed Beads)

» 1 C-clip or S-clip

» 2 looms

» 1 hook

Loom Configuration
Offset/staggered, double

Banding the Beads
Following the instructions on page 26 and matching the bead and band colors, place five seed beads each on thirty bands and then place each of the 30 large beads on a band.

PLACING THE BANDS AND BEADS

1. Position your loom so the red arrow is pointing away from you. Place a large pink beaded band from peg 2 to peg 1, a second from 1 to 4, and a third from 4 to 8.

2. Repeat this on the other side to form a hexagon shape.

3. Place a single pink band from peg 5 to peg 6.

A

B

4. Working in a clockwise direction, place single pink bands from peg 5 to peg 3, 5 to 2, and so on. Steps I through 4 are shown in illustration A.

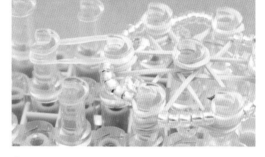

6. Place a single clear band from peg 8 to peg II. Steps 5 and 6 are shown in illustration B.

5. Place a pink cap band on peg 5. Place pink seed beaded bands in the same pattern as the large beaded bands, starting from peg 2 to peg I, I to 4, and 4 to 8, and then repeating on the other side.

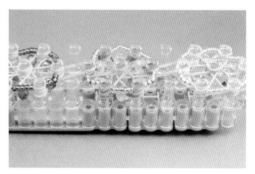

7. Repeat steps I through 6 to make a total of five flowers, each in a different color, first placing the large beaded bands, then the single bands, and then the seed beaded bands for each.

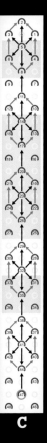

LOOPING THE BANDS

8. After you have made your last flower, place a clear band from peg 44 to peg 47 and add a clear cap band to peg 47. Reposition the loom so the red arrow is pointing toward you. Hook the top band just below the cap band on peg 47 and bring it up and over to peg 44.

10. Hook the next single band below the cap band on peg 41 and bring it up and over to peg 40.

11. Repeat step 10, working around the flower in a counterclockwise pattern. Steps 8 through 12 are shown with black arrows in illustration C.

9. Hook the top single band below the cap band on peg 41 and bring it up and over to peg 44.

12. Hook the second-to-last beaded band on peg 44 and bring it over to peg 42. Hook the bottom beaded band on peg 42 and bring it forward to peg 39. Hook the bottom band on peg 39 and bring it over to peg 38. Repeat on the other side of the flower. This step is shown with blue arrows in illustration C.

13. Grab the bottom clear band on peg 38 and bring it up and over to peg 35. Repeat steps 9 through 12 for the rest of the flowers. (The entire looping sequence is shown in illustration C.) Thread your hook through all the bands on peg 2 and then pull through a single band and loop it around all the bands on that peg. Holding onto that new band, you can remove your bracelet from the loom. Attach a C-clip or S-clip to both sides of the bracelet.

LoomLove.com
Video Tutorial

Beaded Rainbow Blossom Pendant

This pendant is a single "flower" from the Beaded Rainbow Blossoms Bracelet. We used glass seed beads to frame the flower and glass faceted beads for the flower. You can add a jump ring to the pendant, or you just can hang the pendant from the rubber band slip knot.

Level of Difficulty
» Intermediate

What You'll Need
» 6 jelly bands in green

» 6 solid bands dark green

» 8 solid bands teal

» 3 round faceted glass beads in green (The Halcraft Bead Gallery)

» 3 round faceted glass beads in clear (The Halcraft Bead Gallery)

» 30 glass seed beads in green (The Halcraft Bead Gallery)

» 1 loom

» 1 hook

» 1 jump ring (optional)

» Black silk cord

Loom Configuration
Offset/staggered

Banding the Beads
Following the instructions on page 26, place five seed beads each on six green jelly bands and then place each of the six round beads on a dark green band.

PLACING THE BANDS AND BEADS

1. Position your loom so the red arrow is pointing away from you. Place a round green beaded band from peg 2 to peg 1, a dark green band with a clear bead from peg 1 to peg 4, and a round green beaded band from peg 4 to peg 8.

2. Repeat step 1 on the other side to form a hexagon shape, alternating clear and green beads.

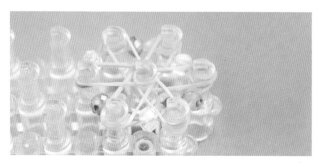

3. Place a single teal band from peg 5 to peg 6. Working in a clockwise direction, place a single teal band from peg 5 to peg 3, 5 to 2, and so on, around the entire flower. Steps 1 through 3 are shown in illustration A.

A

B

C

D

4. Place a teal cap band on peg 5. Place green seed beaded bands in the same pattern as the large beaded bands, starting from peg 2 to peg I, peg I to peg 4, and peg 4 to peg 8, and then repeating on the other side. This step is shown in illustration B.

LOOPING THE BANDS

5. Reposition your loom so the red arrow is pointing toward you. Hook the top band just below the cap band on peg 5 and bring it up and over to peg 8.

LoomLove.com
Video Tutorial

6. Hook the second band below the cap band on peg 5 and bring it up and over to peg 4. Working in a counterclockwise direction, repeat this pattern around the flower. Steps 5 and 6 are shown in illustration C.

7. Hook the second-to-last beaded band on peg 8 and bring it up and over to peg 6. Hook the bottom beaded band on peg 8 and bring it up and over to peg 4.

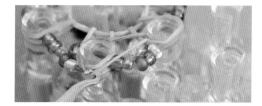

8. Hook the bottom band on peg 6 and bring it up and over to peg 3. Repeat on the other side, bringing the bottom band on peg 4 to peg I. Hook the bottom band on peg 3 and bring it up and over to peg 2. Repeat on the other side, bringing the bottom band on peg I to peg 2. Steps 7 and 8 are shown in illustration D.

9. Remove both seed bead loops from peg 2 by bringing them up and over to rest just behind peg 2.

10. Thread your hook through all of the bands on peg 2 and hook a single band to pull through and loop around all of the bands on that peg. Holding onto that new band, you can remove your pendant from the loom. With both loops on your tool, bring one loop over the other and pull to create a slip knot. Thread the pendant directly onto your cord, or add a jump ring. Tuck in the slip knot in the front of the pendant so it isn't visible. Attach your jump ring to one of the seed beaded bands and thread your cord through the jump ring.

Blue Glow Pendant

For this version of the pendant, we added texture to the inside of the flower by using bubble bands. Use the supplies listed below and follow the instructions on the preceding pages.

Beads and Bands

» 13 solid bands in turquoise

» 7 bubble bands in turquoise

» 6 round faceted glass beads in smoke (Halcraft Bead Gallery)

» 15 glass seed beads in blue (Darcice Japanese Seed Beads)

» 15 glass seed beads in gray (Darcice Japanese Seed Beads)

» Black silk cord

Chandelier Bracelet

The Chandelier Bracelet is made entirely with a hook—no loom. We used pale blue bands and faceted glass beads in matching blue. The uniform color adds a simple elegance to the design. This is the only bracelet design in this book that doesn't require a C-clip or S-clip for finishing.

Level of Difficulty
» Challenging

What You'll Need
» 50 pastel bands in light blue
» 25 round faceted beads in iridescent light blue (dollar store dismantled bracelet)
» 1 hook

Loom Configuration
This project is made off-loom using a hook.

Banding the Beads
Following the instructions on page 26, place all of the beads on the bands.

MAKING THE BRACELET

I. Place both ends of a beaded band on your hook.

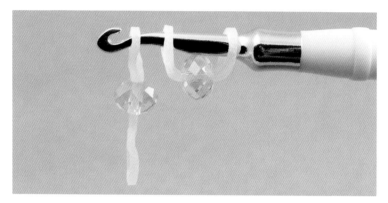

2. Place one end of a second beaded band on your hook.

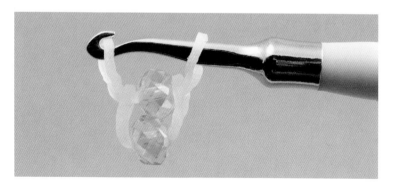

3. Bring both loops of the first beaded band up and over either side of the bead on the second band. Place the other loop of the second beaded band on the hook.

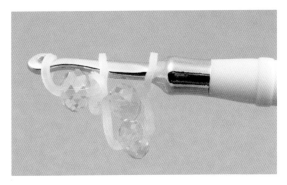

4. Place one end of a third beaded band on the end of the hook. Instead of bringing both bands of the second beaded band onto the new one, only bring one side of the second beaded band onto the third beaded band and bring the other loop of the third beaded band onto the hook. You should now have three loops on your hook.

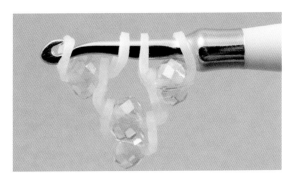

6. Repeat step 4 with a new beaded band.

7. Remove the outer loop and place it on your index finger.

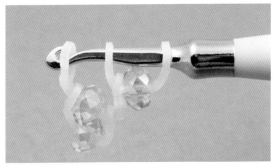

5. While holding on to all three loops, remove them from the hook, flip them over, and place them back on the hook. Your pattern will now be facing in the opposite direction.

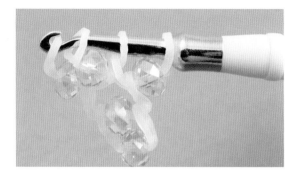

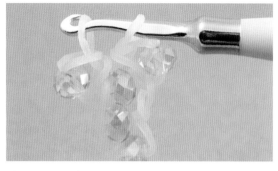

8. Add a new beaded band and bring the two middle loops onto the new band, leaving one remaining on the hook. Place the remaining loop from the new band back onto the hook and then place the loop on your finger back onto the hook.

l0. Add a single band and pull it through all of loops on the hook. Place both ends of the single band on the hook.

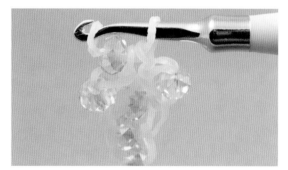

ll. Add a beaded band and pull it through the two loops on the hook. Place both ends of the beaded band on the hook.

9. Move the band on the right side of the middle bead to the left side so that it has a loop on either side.

12. Move the band on the right side of the bead to the left side so that it has a loop on either side.

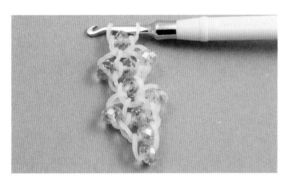

13. Repeat steps 4 through 12 until you've completed the pattern 5 to 6 times. On your last pattern, stop at step 10.

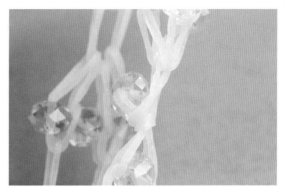

14. You won't need a C-clip for this bracelet. Instead, remove the loops from the hook and place the bands over the first bead. Twist the band twice around the bead to make sure that it's secure.

LoomLove.com
Video Tutorial

Chandelier Earrings

We adapted the Chandelier Bracelet design (see page 120) to create gorgeous earrings that you can make using only your hook. You'll need two French hook earring wires and two jump rings for this project.

Level of Difficulty

» Challenging

What You'll Need

» 25 pastel bands in light blue

» 10 round faceted beads in iridescent light blue (dismantled dollar store bracelet)

» 1 hook

» 2 French hook earring wires

» 2 jump rings

» Chain-nose jewelry pliers

Loom Configuration

This project is made off-loom using a hook.

Banding the Beads

Following the instructions on page 26, place all of the beads on the bands.

MAKING THE EARRINGS

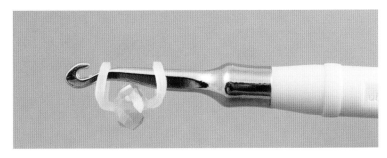

1. Place both loops of a beaded band on your hook.

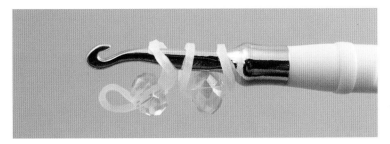

2. Place one loop of a second beaded band on the hook.

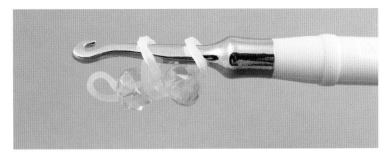

3. Bring the loop of the first beaded band that's closest to the second beaded bead over the second beaded band's loop.

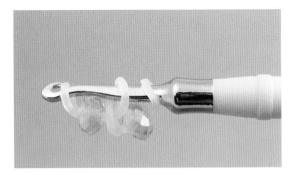

4. Bring the other loop of the second beaded band onto the hook.

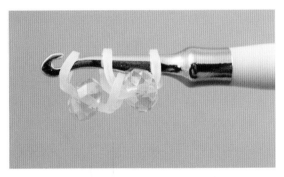

5. You should now have three loops on your hook. While holding on to all three loops, remove them from the hook, flip them over, and place them back on the hook. Your pattern will now be facing in the opposite direction.

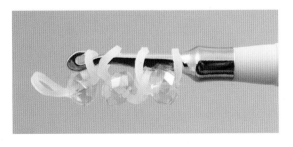

6. Place one loop of a third beaded band on the hook.

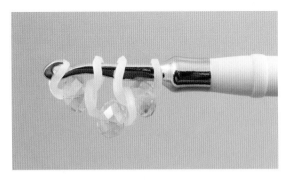

7. Repeat step 3 with a new beaded band.

8. Remove the outer loop and place it on your index finger.

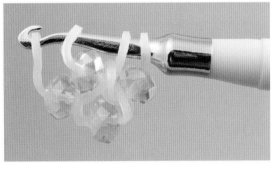

9. Add a new beaded band and bring the two middle loops onto the new band, leaving one remaining on the hook. Place the remaining loop from the new band back onto the hook and then place the loop on your finger back onto the hook.

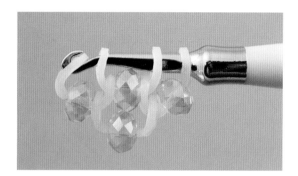

10. Move the band on the right side of the middle bead to the left side so that it has a loop on either side. Place the other end of the unbeaded band back on your hook.

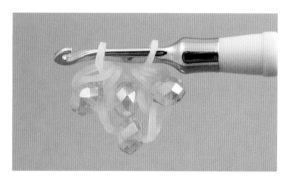

11. Add a single unbeaded band and pull it through all of the loops on the hook, then place both ends of that band on the hook.

12. Add a beaded band and pull it through the two loops on the hook. Place both ends of the beaded band on the hook. Move the band on the right side of the bead to the left side so that it has a loop on either side.

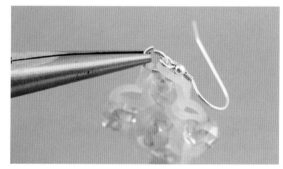

13. Attach a jump ring to the two loops on the hook. Attach an earring hook to the jump ring.

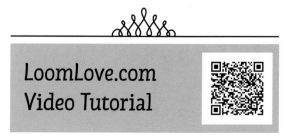

LoomLove.com
Video Tutorial

Bead Garden Bracelet

If you love whimsical designs, you'll fall head over heels for the Bead Garden Bracelet. This fun design is made entirely on a hook. We used a mix of glass seed beads and faceted beads for our version.

Level of Difficulty
» Intermediate

What You'll Need
» 60 solid bands in various shades of blue and aqua, ranging from very light to medium
» 20 solid bands in gray
» 20 faceted round glass in light blue (dismantled dollar store bracelet)
» 40 seed beads in a mix of blue, light blue, and silver (Darice Japanese Seed Beads)
» I hook
» I C-clip or S-clip

Loom Configuration
This project is made off-loom using a hook.

Banding and slip-knotting the beads; making the beaded tassels
Following the instructions on page 26, place all of the beads on the blue bands in various shades. To slip-knot the beads, pull each banded bead through the band to lock it in place. To create a tassel, pull a single gray band through two slip-knotted seed beads and one slip-knotted large faceted bead to gather them together in another slip knot.

MAKING THE BRACELET

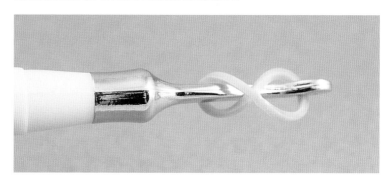

I. Start with a single band of the same color as your first tassel loop. Place it on your hook and twist once so that you have two loops on the hook in a figure eight shape.

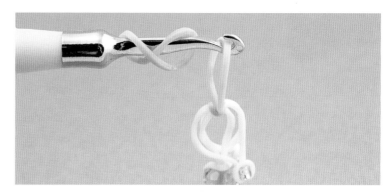

2. Place your first tassel on the end of the hook.

3. Slide the figure eight band onto the tassel loop.

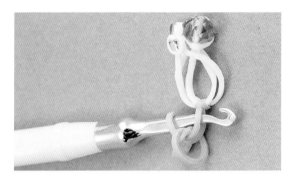

4. Place the other end of the tassel loop onto the hook.

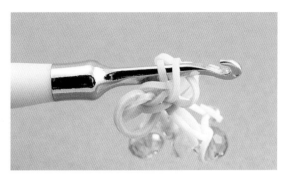

6. Slide both loops on the hook onto the new tassel. Continue this pattern until you have placed all 20 tassels.

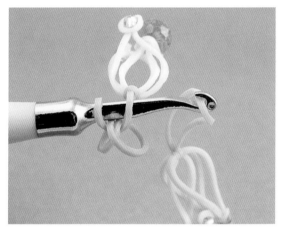

5. Place your second tassel on the end of the hook.

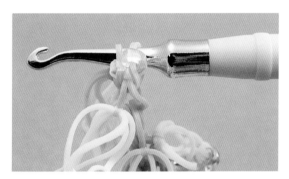

7. When the bracelet fits your wrist, add a C-clip or S-clip to the last two loops on the hook and attach it to the other end of the bracelet.

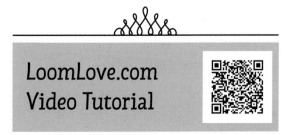

LoomLove.com
Video Tutorial

Cute Coin Purse

The Cute Coin Purse is adorable, and it's also functional. The glass bead closure adds a touch of glam to this creation. You can also add a Beaded Fishtail handle to this design; see page 38 for details.

Level of Difficulty
» Challenging

What You'll Need
» 110 solid bands in white
» 76 solid bands in blue
» 72 solid bands in turquoise
» 4 oval faceted glass beads in clear (Halcraft Bead Gallery)
» 1 loom
» 1 hook
» 1 C-clip or S-clip (optional; required if attaching a Beaded Fishtail handle, which is made separately; see page 38 for details)

Loom Configuration
Rectangular/even, with center row and large blue base removed. The two remaining rows of pegs face in opposite directions.

Banding the Beads
Following the instructions on page 26, place all of the beads on the blue bands.

MAKING THE PURSE

1. Position your loom horizontally, with the red arrow pointing to the right. Place a white band in a figure eight from peg 5 to peg 4 and another in a figure eight pattern from peg 3 to peg 6. This will form an X.

2. Continue this X pattern for the length of the loom, with the next X starting from peg 7 to peg 6 and peg 5 to peg 8 and so on. Your last X will end on the second to last pegs on the loom, peg 23 and peg 24. Steps 1 and 2 are shown in illustration A.

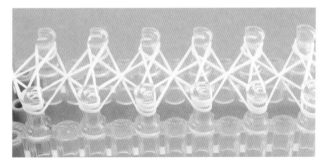

3. Place white bands in a figure eight from peg 3 to peg 4, peg 5 to peg 6, and so on, until you place your last band from peg 23 to peg 24. This step is shown in illustration B.

A

B

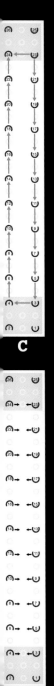

C

D

4. Place a white band from peg 23 to peg 24; this will not be in the figure eight pattern. Place a band from peg 24 to peg 22, another from peg 22 to peg 20, and continue up the loom to peg 3.

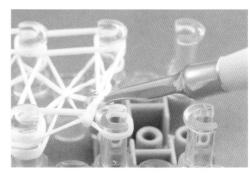

6. Hook the two bottom figure eight bands from peg 23 and lift them up and over the peg toward the center of the loom.

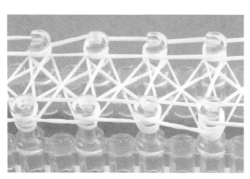

5. Place a white band from peg 3 to peg 4 and continue working up the loom vertically as you did before from peg 3 to peg 5, peg 5 to peg 7, and so on. Steps 4 and 5 are shown in illustration C.

7. Continue with all figure eight bands on each peg; you should have three bands to lift for each peg. Steps 6 and 7 are shown in illustration D.

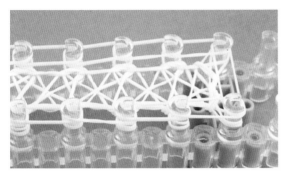

8. To start your next row, place a white band from peg 23 to peg 24, peg 24 to peg 22, and then up the side and around the loom as in step 4.

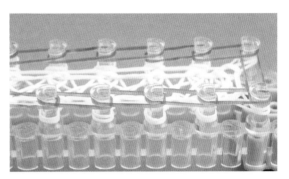

10. You have now completed two rows, and you will repeat steps 4 through 6 for a total of 16 rows. (This means you have 14 left to do.) Add a new color every two rows.

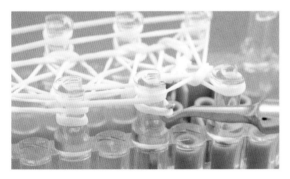

9. Hook the two bottom bands on each peg up and over as in step 6. However, you will only grab two bands, instead of three, on each peg this time.

11. Use your hook to go down through the bands on peg 24 and grab the bottom band and bring it through and across to peg 23.

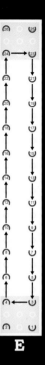

E

12. Grab the bottom band on peg 23 and bring it up and across to peg 21. Continue to work around the loom, grabbing the bottom band and bringing it forward. End on peg 24. Steps 11 and 12 are shown in illustration E.

14. To attach beads for the closure, thread your hook through the top layer of bands. Pull one end of a beaded band through the top layer and thread the other end of the band onto your hook.

13. Use your hook to thread through all of the bands on peg 3 and hook a single band to pull through and loop around all of the bands on that peg. Bring the bottom band over the top band on your hook to create a slip knot. You can now remove the purse from the loom.

15. Pull the first loop over the second to make a slip knot and pull tight. Wrap the excess loop you have from your slip knot around the bead several times.

16. To add a closure, find the loop in the same spot opposite the bead and add a slip knot with a solid band doubled like a cap band. Add beads and closures every other loop.

17. To hide your slip knot loop, thread through a few bands with your hook and pull it through.

Optional: To attach a bracelet for carrying your purse, thread the hook through a few loops on the side of your slip knot on your purse. Remove the cap band side of the bracelet from the C-clip or S-clip and pull it through the loops on your purse, using the hook. Pull the entire bracelet through the loop and add the C-clip or S-clip back onto the bracelet.

LoomLove.com
Video Tutorial

Let's BAND TOGETHER

Making a Difference

Rubber band bracelets aren't just fun to make; they're a perfect way to make a difference!

Kids all around the world have used their bracelets to make a positive difference in the lives of others. Whether it's by selling bracelets to raise money for a favorite charity, raising money to help a friend or loved one in need, or giving their loom creations to others, kids are finding ways to have fun and to be a force for positive change at the same time.

Mia LeRoux, for instance, was only eight years old when she founded LoomsforLove.org, a nonprofit organization dedicated to spreading cheer in hospitals and nursing homes. Mia and her friends create Rainbow Loom bracelets and handmade cards, which they hand-deliver to the residents of those facilities. Mia has inspired kids across the country to do the same. Her goal is to grow a nationwide community of caring children who do good deeds and recognize the impact that they can have by working together.

Seven-year-old "SuperMax" Wilford, a boy fighting brain cancer, founded MaxLoveProject.org, a nonprofit organization working to help SuperKids thrive against cancer and other life-threatening conditions. Max appeared on *Jimmy Kimmel Live* in 2014. During the show, Kimmel sported a "Suit of the Loom" made from loom creations that viewers submitted to the show. The suit was auctioned off and purchased by Choon Ng, the inventor of Rainbow Loom, for $40,000. The money raised went toward fighting childhood cancers. The MaxLoveProject has also held several successful Loom-a-thons, raising money and awareness for their cause.

There are other ways to make a difference with your loom bracelets aside from selling them. Loom Love raised a total of $800 for a local animal rescue group by creating and selling Rainbow Loom-themed Valentines. You could also host a loom party and ask everyone who attends to bring a canned good that you can then donate to your local food bank. You could also donate your bracelets to a cause. AHOPE, for instance, an organization that provides free assistance for housing, clothing, schooling, medical care and other needs to HIV-positive orphans in Ethiopia, created the Rainbow Loom project, which involved collecting loom bracelets and giving them to children in Ethiopia. Other charity organizations have run similar projects.

Loom creations also make thoughtful gifts. Got a fabulous uncle or an adorable aunt? Is your grandma the best? What about a special cousin who lives far away? Make their day by sending them one of your bracelets in the mail, along with a handwritten note.

Another option is to purchase loom supplies for someone who can't afford them. Many charities are in search of toys to give to needy kids. We purchased several loom cases and filled them with bands to give to our local youth center.

Last, but not least, you can give back by sharing your loom skills with others. If you've mastered a new pattern or skill—for example, how to add beads to your projects—pass on your knowledge to others.

Selling Your Bracelets

Saving up for something special? Maybe you're saving money for more loom supplies. If so, why not sell some of your *Rubber Band Glam* creations? Purchase a booth at your local craft fair or simply sell them to your friends and family. Make sure you factor in the cost of the bands and the beads when determining the selling price for your bracelets.

Another option is to sell your creations online. Etsy and Artfire are just two online sites that allow you to sell handmade wares. Etsy requires you to pay a nominal listing fee for each item, and it also takes a small percentage when an item sells. Artfire requires you pay a monthly fee rather than a listing fee and a commission. Keep in mind that the competition on these online marketplaces is fierce; you'll need to have great photos, stellar descriptions, and lots of inventory, along with a solid social media plan to do well on these platforms.

Starting a Loom Meet-Up

Why not get together with other loomers and share new designs by starting a loom meet-up at your school or in your neighborhood? Post flyers or use social media to spread the word. You might even find an enthusiastic teacher or other community leader to help you organize the group.

Loom meet-ups are a great way to spend time with friends and meet new ones. Also, they give you the opportunity to improve your looming skills and to share those skills with others.

Resources

Video Links

In addition to scanning the QR codes that appear at the end of each project, you can also access the LoomLove.com video tutorials by typing into your browser either www.loomlove.com or www.quarrybooks.com/pages/rubberbandglam, then the name of the project as shown below:

/Beadazzled

/Beaded-Fishtail-Bracelet

/Beaded-Fishtail-Dangles

/Bead-Garden

/Beaded-Ladder

/Beaded-Lantern

/Beaded-Rainbow-Blossoms-Bracelet

/Beaded-Rainbow-Blossom-Pendant

/Beaded-Single

/Beaded-Triple-Single

/Chandelier-Bracelet

/Chandelier-Earrings

/Crystal-Wave

/Cute-Coin-Purse

/Diamond-Eyes

/Gem-Flower-Bracelet

/Gem-Flower-Hairclip

/Gem-Flower-KeyChain

/Illumine

/Jane-Austen

/Shimmer

/Sparkle-Square

/Spring-Bouquet

/Starglow

/Whirlwind

YouTube Channels

Go to www.youtube.com and search for these channels to find more looming tutorials.

Loom Love

AmandaandMonica Rloomy

Cheryl Mayberry

Claire's Wears

Cortney Nicole

Craft Life

Crafty Ladybug Creations

DIY Mommy

Elegant Fashion 360

Emily Hill

Feelinspiffy

Izzalicious Designs

Jays Alvarez

Jordantinel

Justin's Toys

Looming WithCheryl

LoominLooney

Lovely Lovebird Designs

Loves2Loom

Lumefinity

Made by Mommy

MarloomZ Creations

Olivia's Looms and Crafts

PG's Loomacy

Rainbow Loom

Rena T

Sae wolfe

Suzanne H-B

TheParentingChannel

TutorialsByA

YarnJourney

Books

Epic Rubber Band Crafts by Colleen Dorsey

Loom Band It!: 60 Rubber Band Projects for the Budding Loomineer by Kat Roberts and Tessa Sillars-Powell

Loom Magic!: 25 Awesome, Never-Before-Seen Designs for an Amazing Rainbow of Projects by John McCann and Becky Thomas

The Loomatic's Interactive Guide to the Rainbow Loom by Suzanne M. Peterson

Totally Awesome Rubber Band Jewelry by Colleen Dorsey

Supplies

Amazon
www.amazon.com

Jo-Ann
www.joann.com

Learning Express Toys
www.learningexpress.com

Mastermind Toys
www.mastermindtoys.com

Michaels
www.michaels.com

Official Rainbow Loom USA Webstore
www.rainloom.com

About the Authors

Christina Friedrichsen-Truman, along with her daughters Emily and Madeline Truman, are the founders of LoomLove.com, which has received more than 6 million visitors from around the world.

Mother-daughter bonding time doesn't just include making rubber band bracelets; the Loom Love ladies have a fondness for just about anything that involves paint, glue, or glitter.

When they are not dreaming up nifty craft projects, they can be spotted at area thrift stores and yard sales searching for vintage treasures or scouring the local beaches for sea glass and lucky stones. They live just outside of Windsor, Ontario, Canada, with Darin Truman, the tech guy behind LoomLove.com (Christina's husband and Emily and Maddie's dad), and their menagerie of pets.

Acknowledgments

We are so grateful for the support we have received from our fans at LoomLove.com who continue to encourage us with their enthusiasm.

The Rainbow Loom community of creators is also a constant source of inspiration for us. We are truly in awe of all of the talent that has surfaced because of this incredible craft.

Finally, we'd like to give a shout out to the team at Quarry Books who worked countless hours to assist us in bringing our loom creations to life in book form.

Index